"Mastering Your Website"

The Insider's Guide To Fully
Understanding Your Website, Search
Engine Optimization and Building Your
Brand Online

John Colascione

ISBN-10: 1475155662
ISBN-13: 978-1475155662

Searchen Networks Inc.
President, John Colascione
5 Ketridge Street
West Babylon, New York, 11704
www.searchen.com

Manufactured in the United States of America.

The logo and terms "SEARCHEN" ® and "SEARCHEN NETWORKS" ® are registered trademarks of Searchen Networks Inc., in the United States.

Cover Design: Bantech Solutions
Cover Illustration: Bantech Solutions
Cover © 2012 Searchen Networks Inc.
Printed in the U.S.A.

A copy of this book is on file with the Library of Congress.

ISBN-10: 1475155662
ISBN-13: 978-1475155662

Dedication

This book is dedicated to **my wife Denise** *who believed in me throughout all of the ups and downs of my Internet marketing career. For never groaning over late nights, big dreams, missed events and eighteen (18) hour days at my desk in "the chair". Only she and I will truly understand the meaning of the quote: "Hey Babe, look at that – it's almost a dollar a day!"*

Thanks also to my brother Sal, for inspiring me to purchase my very first domain name.

And my three wonderful children, Dominic Michael, Giavanna Rose, and Michael John.

Praise for the Author

"I think I've said before, I've always avidly read what you've written and admired what you've done. To get your seal of approval means a lot!" – Jeffrey Behrendt Esq., InForum.in

"This is one of the most informative guides on beginning website marketing and should be required reading for all new store owners. It has a thorough presentation of search engine and algorithm basics as well as some more advanced theories. Highly recommended reading!" - Robert R. "Bobby" Easland Jr. (Chemo) osCommerce Specialist

"WOW John, My AdSense revenue is way up...three times in fact after I applied your suggestion. Thanks Brother for the added mullah...lol." - Doug Holland (BigDoug), Branson Critique

"What a really useful site you have. I am stunned that someone has gone to all that trouble to help others. I have learned a great deal as a result of reading your advice." - Melissa

"John Colascione was instrumental in the development and search engine marketing of our web site since the beginning. It was nothing short of a miracle that our site has been able to survive some significant changes, and John's experience has been our secret weapon." - Tony Sena, Shelter Realty Inc.

"I had a chance to check out the info on the link that you sent me, I am very impressed! Thanks for the help with getting this new site up and going." - Brian Keegan, Quick Cash Auto, Inc.

"John, thank you for this article. It was well written informative and inspiring. It is people like you that motivate us to keep moving forward and keep our dreams alive." - Juan Gutierrez

Table of Contents

Preface

For over a decade I have been researching changes in search engines and how they affect a scope of platforms available to consumers. Much of this time has been spent evaluating each individual search engine, its algorithms, comparing them with changes in web site architecture, and the differences that those particular changes have on a web sites overall visibility within search results.

I genuinely enjoy helping people learn and understand the Internet. What really works, what worked for me, and what (in my opinion) not to waste time on.

Over the years, I've had more than a few people approach me and say, "Hey, I have this great idea for a web site, how do I get started?" I've kept it no secret that I have been very successful at creating and marketing web sites on the Internet, so putting this question to me is not unusual at all for those who know me. What I have found is that there just isn't one simple answer. I'll often reply "Well, first you need to register a domain name so you have something to start with and then afterwards you can work on building a web site".

Although I have answered their question with a very true and accurate response, I know they have not a clue where to get started and what is really involved in starting a web site - and actually getting it to be successful. Anyone can register a domain name, but what do you do next? I mean, what good is having a web site if no one is ever going to see it? I just sort of point them in the right direction hoping they'll eventually find their way. But I know deep down that they've got to start off on the right foot for things to actually materialize. Knowledge is the absolute key to running a business online. This is precisely why a news blogger can be just as influential as the New York Times. It's not about having money and deep pockets. It's about having the knowledge you need to become a success and develop a winning strategy; without it you're really just dead in the water.

This book is, by no stretch, an all-encompassing guide to owning a web site. It is short, but it is informative. Most importantly, though, if you have little or no idea of what to expect when starting your web site, this book is UNDERSTANDABLE.

Introduction

M y name is John Colascione, President and Chief Executive Officer of Searchen Networks ® Inc., an Internet Marketing and Search Engine Consultancy headquartered in West Babylon, New York, on Long Island.

About twelve years ago when I first started with the Internet, I didn't know much at all about having a web site let alone making or marketing one. I was a regular AOL user and I dabbled a little here and there to look things up and check email. I don't even think many people really knew what Google was back then (Google began in January 1996) and search engines were far from a common tool or thought for the average person.

I was a truck driver by trade and held my CDL (Commercial Driver's License). Although I had a regular "*job*" like everyone else, driving trucks allowed me to be on my own and do my own thing. It also paid the bills and gave me some peace in my day to do things my way. I lived in the suburbs of New York on Long Island where the cost of living was higher than average and those wanting the finer things in life don't see them come easy. It was time to find a trade I enjoyed which I could turn into a business of my own in order to get ahead and I was willing to do whatever it was going to take to get it going.

I wound up taking a class for computers at Hendricks Institute of Technology in Lindenhurst, New York. There I broke the ice using the computer taking a course to become a Microsoft Certified Systems Engineer (MCSE). Troubleshooting operating systems wasn't for me and I left the class before taking the test, but my dabbling with computers and the Internet was far from over.

I continued with what I already knew about the net (which wasn't much). I started using EBay to buy hard to find collectibles only to resell them on that same venue for 2 to 3 times what I paid for them. I built my first web site using a site builder program I found from Godaddy.com. Although the program was great, I reverse engineered it through a significant desire to understand how it worked so that I didn't need it anymore; I wanted to do it on my own steam. After I built one site, I started to build more.

Eventually I realized that I needed to get lots of people to find my sites otherwise I would be the only one using them and I didn't have much money to advertise through radio or television. I began thinking of how I found stuff online with search engines. If only I could get search engines to return my sites to the top of the results I would probably "have it made" and it wouldn't really cost much at all other than some time to figure out how that works; why some sites pop up where they do. The rest is history.

Today, I happily own and maintain several online businesses which I created from the ground up. I also collect and invest in domain names and play a key role in the online businesses of others. I consistently receive offers to partner in exchange for my expertise and assistance but although I'd love to be a part of all of them, there is only so much time in a day and I can only spread myself so thin.

I mostly enjoy building online businesses at the initial stages, creating the model. There is something about making something from nothing that is really fulfilling. I like to do everything my own way until it comes time to get others involved to help run the business when (and if) things take off. Not every idea works and there is much trial and error involved in any business, but as an entrepreneur it is entirely up to you to go through that process of hit and miss with your endeavors.

If I have learned one monumental thing throughout all of this which I can pass on to you first and foremost, it surely is to not spread yourself too thin. Don't try to be a winner at a million different web sites. Stay focused and put everything you've got into one project until it works. It takes a lot of determination and passion to make something truly fantastic come about. You have to give it your all to make it work and become a hit. I've always found that the projects I worked on the most panned out the best, and I know that's just not a coincidence.

So, whatever site you plan to run or build, make sure it involves something you enjoy and are passionate about – because that's how you become a winner at it. You've got to find your niche and absolutely dominate it by learning everything you can, building a great plan, that puts your web site to work for you, instead of you for it.

Chapter 1 (Getting Your Domain Name)

In the beginning, which I call it, things were much simpler yet not so different than they are now. Entrepreneurs still need a place to start, and that starting point is your idea, your businesses name, and its brand which will be built from long hours of grueling hard work and dedicated effort towards a new enterprise.

Starting a business is an exciting experience, but its success is that much more exhilarating. When you're getting into your first, second or even third great idea, it's important to be aware that most small businesses fail within their first year. This is because many people lose the drive needed to turn an idea into action or otherwise a successful business. This is what separates the true entrepreneur from the *"dreamer"*. Not giving up, sticking with it when others would have walked away. That's the difference. I call these people *"doers"*. Are you a doer?

Many people I talk to just don't realize how easy it is to buy that little piece of pie in the sky. That web name that captures someone's creativity. The .com starting point. Some think it's very expensive to buy a domain or you need some sort of technical ability to get one. This couldn't be further from the reality of it all.

Did you know that you can buy a domain name for as little as about $10.00 giving you rights to the name for a full year? Did you know these names can be forwarded anywhere you like easily through domain name forwarding, a service commonly provided free from the registrar you buy from (provided you use a good registrar service)? Most people I know, surprisingly, don't. The idea of buying their domain name just slipped through the cracks, it's left for the web guy to worry about, or thought about last. I think about this first before I start any business. If I don't like the name, it's over before I even get started.

The net is such an important part of any business - but it's competitive! And you need to get your feet on the ground right from the start for it to work, but the net is surely where it's at. Just ask Verizon ® or Yellowbook®. These companies have completely changed their entire way of doing business - and not because they wanted to either.

Small businesses these days have a better understanding of the importance of having a web site to compete in this new internet-savvy space. Companies who have tried to delay their move towards the Internet are warming up to the fact that if your business is not online - you're very likely to go out of business in the near future. This is why there has never been a better time than right now to learn and understand the ins and outs of how your business will compete, thrive, or just stay alive.

Reselling a domain name could also yield huge profits. Domain name reselling has expanded, and many domain resellers are now stand-alone internet businesses. Domain name auctions can provide a reseller with a means to buy and sell premium domains, and a savvy investor can build a successful business around the right generic domain properties. It is not out-of-the-norm for a name to be purchased for just $10.00 and resold at a later date for tens of thousands of dollars. Good names are running out fast. On average over 100,000 .com domain names are registered every 24 hours. Registering a domain is done in a few steps.

1. You need to search and find a domain name which can be done at https://www.searchen.com. Using this site you can key in possible names and the system will tell you if they are available for purchase. You'll also be presented with premium names which are more expensive. You don't need to buy them. Keep trying until you find a great name that is available to the public so you can grab it for under $10.00.

2. You'll need to create a domain name customer account. This will be your online interface which will allow you to control your domain, keep it registered and control domain forwarding or other free features provided. Your domain account username and password should be kept with the upmost privacy and security as they are the "*keys*" to your internet castle.

3. You'll need to pay for your domain by credit card or PayPal if you prefer. You'll be presented with several options for the length of registration period. The maximum registration period that can be purchased at one time is 10 years. Although you can register for as little as one year, I always recommend registering for multiple years, but the choice is up to you.

The buyer of a domain name needs to understand that domain name ownership comes with an agreement with the domain name service provider and that a domain contract may have several stipulations which the buyer should read carefully.

Generally, an Internet domain name is leased on a yearly basis and it is important that the buyer understand that failing to renew such domain could cause serious loss or hardship to an Internet business. Domain buyers should understand that it is in his/her best interest to review the domain name service agreement once a domain name is purchased.

Often a web site owner loses touch with their web site designer or for some reason the web designer irresponsibly allows the name to expire which can spiral a web business into absolute chaos. I have seen this happen so many times. This is why I always recommend a business owner be educated about their own domain name and preferably is the one to control their domain and/or at minimum have full access to the domain name account. People part ways, service providers go out of business, email addresses change or people just otherwise lose touch after a number of years. This is why you should *always* be well informed about the access and control of your domain.

When you're doing business online, your domain name will serve as your location, your store front, your place on the web where consumers can find whatever it is that you're offering them. Your domain will represent a lot of things, but most importantly, your domain name will represent your web presence.

Having a great domain name for your business is very important, so take the time to choose it wisely as you'll likely not change the name once you've gotten started. Whatever it is that you're going to do, make certain to start with a name that is easy to remember, and won't likely be confused with other domains. Also try to include keywords in your domain and consider purchasing the .net and .org version of whichever .com you choose. Your domain name will help build traffic - the hottest commodity on the web. It can be the difference between having a store set back off the road with no signs on a dead end street, or one on the corner of a busy intersection where traffic thrives day in and day out.

Remember this:

- Try to get a .com, and the shorter the better.
- If it has keywords in it, it's a plus – *(see page 42)*: (keywordcompany.com, keywordservices.com)
- Purchase your brand name and consider buying variations, plurals or synonyms of your domain(s).
- Consider buying other popular extensions like .net or .org to protect your brand.

Chapter 2 (Why Do I Need Web Hosting?)

The buyer of a domain name should understand that Internet web sites require web hosting, and that any web hosting service requires an agreement with a web hosting service provider. You can point (forward) your domain name anywhere you like for free, but if you're turning it into a live web site, get ready to look into web hosting. Most of the time your domain name service provider will also offer web hosting services. In this case, a buyer of a domain at https://www.searchen.com can add affordable and reliable web hosting services. The hosting contract may also contain many stipulations for service and the buyer should be aware that he/she should take the time to read and learn about these agreements. Typically web hosting can be purchased on a month to month basis or paid yearly. This is an extra expense in running a web site but it is a relatively low expense depending on the functions of web site. For instance, a five page web site could cost as little as $5.00 per month to host verses a large classifieds site or social network with user posting, data storage, and backup requirements which could require a dedicated machine for $800.00 a month or more - It greatly depends on the site you intend to run and yourself or the staff you've got to help you manage it.

The most popular web hosting platforms are either Windows or Linux. Most web hosting companies' offer both but my personal preference has always been Linux.

When you pay for web hosting it's usually on a monthly basis and it serves as a location on the Internet to store all of the files which make up your site. It's basically a space you rent to store and allow access to your site and data. It usually includes access to email and other portions of your site which depend on hosting. When you purchase a web hosting space, depending on the site, it's similar to purchasing an apartment in an apartment building. You're allowed access to one apartment within the building and you're allowed to have guests. You have to pay the rent (fee) each month in order to have access and allow access to others. The larger the space and the more guests you have the more area you require. It's the same thing with web hosting. As long as you pay the bill, access to your area is available; provided that your account remains current, don't disturb anyone else and follow the rules, you won't get evicted.

Choosing a Web Hosting Provider

Choosing a web hosting provider is a very important process. It's also, in addition to your domain, is a foundation on which your business will run. Generally speaking, the more you pay, the better the service.

Most popular web hosting services provide good service and most guarantee at least a 99% uptime. This means that they guarantee that 99% of the time, your hosting service will be running, available, uninterrupted and error free. The differences between hosting companies is mostly about support. Most offer 24/7/365 day support, which means they're available any time day or night, even on holidays. Never choose a company who doesn't offer a 24/7/365 schedule; if your site goes down you don't want to have to wait till they come back to work for assistance. Having your site down for any amount of time means lost traffic, lost revenue and possibly even lost rankings in search engines from inaccessibility of your site. Only choose a web hosting service which offers 24/7/365 day support.

Another significant difference in web hosting service providers is in the way in which they deliver support. Some companies will only provide support through a web based ticket system which is similar to emailing them. Some do not offer phone support for technical issues related to web hosting. I would steer clear of this as well. You want a hosting provider who will pick up the phone and have technicians available for yourself or your webmaster to troubleshoot problems which may arise. Hosting providers only offering ticket support can make things difficult and time consuming if and when you need to resolve problems. It is always better to choose a web hosting service that provides both ticket and live phone support. Take it from me, I've learned from experience. With the wrong hosting company you could be up all night submitting and answering tickets.

Lastly, there are choices of control panels offered with web hosting services. Both Plesk and CPanel are extremely popular web hosting control panels. CPanel is probably the best, easiest and most widely used control panel and it is very easy to use or learn to use for a new user. Your control panel is where you'll administrate your hosting. If you have a choice between Plesk and CPanel choose CPanel. It'll probably be the easiest to get started with. Additionally, if you require a webmaster or any assistant to work on your site, they are more likely to be familiar with a CPanel hosting account.

Chapter 3 (Building & Running a Web Site)

Entrepreneurs planning on running a web business need to understand that taking control of an Internet web site to develop and run as an Internet business, like any other business, is not always easy, and that there could be technical difficulties encountered which are likely to cause added expenses or require technical personnel to repair, maintain and/or administrate. The entire risk of making an Internet business work and/or become profitable enough to maintain these additional costs rests entirely with the creator.

When I began this exciting journey years ago I learned everything I needed to know right from the Internet and forums where people had the same creativity and willingness to share information with me as I do with you here. If you have questions about what you're really up against in different situations or anything else relative to building your business online you're going to find what you need to make it happen in this book, but you're also going to learn a lot along the way.

Running an Internet business isn't always easy, and in some cases, it's a responsibility. Depending on the site you run and the service you provide, there could be many people depending on what it is you do. Successful Internet businesses usually begin with a strong footing and savvy owner – someone who knows the ins and outs of what to do and what not to do. If you're running a classifieds site, the ability for users to visit and place an ad rests entirely with you. If they come visit your site and it is down, under construction or otherwise unavailable, they may never return. Remember, your Internet business will run 24 hours per day, 7 days per week and yes on Christmas too.

I often find myself telling a story of how I used to not sleep at night because of the company I decided to work with for web hosting. I spent hours upon hours and many sleepless nights submitting support tickets and dealing with web site hosting issues which took down my site. Many times I would wake and my sites were down. I finally realized and learned the hard way that my sites were outgrowing their host and if I wanted better support I needed to find another provider. Eventually I made the move and transferred my sites. It was great to sleep again. Now if and when my sites go down the hosting provider usually knows about it first and it's often automatically fixed while I sleep. I wake to notification that things were down, but have been repaired through the night. This is dedicated and fully managed hosting service at work, but keep in mind that the smaller the hosting account and the lesser the fee, the less likely this level of service will be provided. Again, try to choose the right host for you; if your site is going to be very busy, don't just consider price, consider service.

Will You Require A Webmaster?

Being involved in an Internet business for quite some time, I have had many instances where I've explained why exactly it is that you should have a webmaster or web maintenance service if your site is complex. If you are running an online business there are a few things you need to understand. Once you begin to add functionality to a website, it becomes more of a responsibility and a worry than your ordinary five page info only web site. As soon as you start adding programming to your site in PHP, ASP, etc., you begin to create what I call "*doors*". Once these doors are installed you must always make sure the doors remain locked. Vandals will try to unlock these doors, or "break in" to your web site or web server (hosting account).

In most cases they do this to access your server to send spam email. Sometimes they just do it for fun. They are "*hackers*" and they really just want to break your things. These programming systems which are sometimes classifieds, forums, shopping carts, etc., become a problem because of hackers, especially if you are storing credit cards or other secure data. Each manufacturer must update their versions of software when new hacks or vulnerabilities are discovered. Sometimes vulnerability requires an upgrade. Sometimes your modifications need to be done over. It's never a set it and forget it scenario.

Once you add functionality to a website, you must pay more attention to what is happening on the server and always be making sure that no-one is opening the doors. Another point that seems to be misunderstood is the fact that your data is valuable. If you have a shopping cart, it's important to have a webmaster (or yourself) keeping an eye on things. Let's go through an example of not keeping an eye on things and what could go wrong.

Let's say you have created your site, you have a shopping cart and everything is up and working and sales are coming in, but no-one is watching the site itself, you know the technical stuff. You figure "I bought the site and do not need much of anything else". You'll just send the orders out when they come in. Business is good, you've got nothing to worry about, right? So one day the orders stop coming. You notice this for a few days in a row, then a week and things seem terrible all of the sudden. I mean, sales have dropped dramatically. Not even one single order in a few weeks now. So you finally go to check the web site to see what's wrong – bang – no web site! The site is just gone.

You do a little checking into things and discover that your credit card was expired, and the guy that built the site and set it up wasn't checking his email or for whatever reason failed to let you know (probably because he didn't care). The entire website including the database which stores all the products and order data is gone! The hosting account was 60 days overdue and after several emails the hosting company finally just cancelled the account. Even the database was erased.

Here is where we begin to understand the value of data as well as having a certain level of expertise and responsibility attached to your internet business. Every order that was placed, every customer email that was saved, every product that was photographed, gone. Now you may be thinking that surely there must be backups, where are the backups? Strike two. The webmaster never configured the hosting set-up to include back-ups, and the hosting company, being that the account was 60 days past due, deleted the account.

The point I'm trying to make here in this example is that once you decide to go into business on the Internet, it is very important to take it seriously. You've got to cover every base, think of every scenario and _keep your eyes on the ball!_ Like anything else, what you put into the business, is what you'll get out of it.

I did have to explain this very situation to someone after it happened to them which is why I am adding it here. Don't let something like this happen to you. Know your web site, understand its needs, and learn to always back-up data. It is important to have someone very knowledgeable to help you cover the bases. If you're going it on your own take the time to evaluate your systems, your site, it's requirements and how to keep what you've put into it, in almost any scenario.

Website Builder Programs

If you're looking to build a web site but you do not wish to learn how to build more than one or two, you can consider using a simple website builder program which will allow you to simply drag, drop, click and build your website right online. Again, I began with a website builder program but I wanted to go much further, so I wanted to learn how to build them from scratch and make my own custom graphics.

A website builder program is the easiest way to build your own site without having to purchase any expensive software or hire a web designer. Website builder programs are designed to be simple and usually include web hosting, galleries of stock images, various web templates to choose from and do not require much work publishing your site to Internet. You just sort of design (click, drag, drop and insert) it in a simple designer interface and there is usually a button to "preview" and "publish" your works to the web. When you like what you see in the preview you finalize it.

You can find one here: *http://sitebuilder.searchen.com*

Adobe Dreamweaver

Adobe Dreamweaver is a software application available for both Mac and Windows operating systems. The software supports building web sites with CSS, JavaScript, and various server-side scripting languages including HTML, ASP and PHP. You'll need this software (or something very much like it) to build your web pages and publish your files to your hosting account if you want to code them up yourself as well as have complete control over the look and feel of your site. It can also be used to write your own scripts and custom programming.

Adobe Dreamweaver is all you need to build your web site from scratch provided that you are not editing and/or creating custom graphics. It will take a little time for you to get the hang of how to use it, but it is well worth the time, energy and money for the software – even if you are only managing one site but you want total and full control of the look and feel. It allows you to create, write and edit web based files, connect to your hosting account and place the files on the server. Files are pushed up and pulled down and there are many excellent features for working with large sites like "find and replace" which can make changes to hundreds or thousands of files at one time and only upload or overwrite the ones you've changed.

Personally, I wouldn't want to manage a web site, especially a large or complex one, without having a copy of Adobe Dreamweaver.

You can get a copy here:
http://www.adobe.com/products/dreamweaver/

Adobe Photoshop (or ImageReady)

Adobe Photoshop is a graphics editing program for image editing available for both Mac and Windows operating systems. Photoshop has the ability to read and write image formats such as .PSD, .EPS, .PNG, .GIF, and .JPEG. You'll need this if you want to edit photos and create graphics for your site. If you can still find it, I actually prefer Adobe ImageReady over Photoshop, as it is easier to use for beginners, but it was discontinued in 2007, so Photoshop may be required.

You can get a copy here: <u>*http://adobe.com/photoshop*</u>

WordPress

WordPress is a free content management system (CMS) based on PHP programming and a MySQL database. It has many features including a plug-in architecture and a template system which controls the look and feel of WordPress. There are thousands of free and paid templates available and you do not need to do any coding when using WordPress, but if you know how you'll get slightly more out of it. About 22% of all new sites run on WordPress and it is currently the most popular CMS in use on the Internet.

WordPress requires web hosting and runs very well with most basic hosting accounts with either Plesk or Cpanel control panels. After installing it most everything can be administrated through the administrator control panel, including content, images, pages, plug-ins, templates, software and security updates from WordPress.

You can download a free copy here: <u>*http://wordpress.org*</u>

FTP Access: Connecting to Your Web Host

It may seem quite mundane to some, but I would like to cover FTP access in this chapter as you'll have trouble doing much to your site without using it or at least knowing what it is (in most web hosting environments) and I see it as one of the first issues that could become confusing or complicated to some – possibly enough to stop you in your tracks.

FTP is short for "**File Transfer Protocol**", a standard network protocol used to transfer files from one host (your computer) to another host (your hosting server) over a network, such as the Internet.

This is the process which you will likely use to connect to your web server and upload your web site on the Internet. Some hosting services have restrictions on how they allow you to connect, but most will require this info in a similar manner as shown below.

Using a program like Adobe Dreamweaver, or similar FTP software, you'll need the following information to connect to your web server:

1. The IP Address (location of server, usually looks like this 125.34.56.107).

2. The root directory (the folder on your server where your files will go).
3. Your FTP username (a username is required to connect).
4. Your FTP password (a password is required to connect).

The FTP information comes from your hosting company, either by them sending it to you when you purchase the account or you login to a system and create it.

Either way, you'll likely need your FTP connection details to connect to your hosting space and upload the files which make up your web site. In most cases, you can start to build your web site with just a few files (.html) and images (.jpg,.gif).

The only other thing you'll need is your web hosting providers' name servers (the DNS). In order to point your domain name to your web hosting, you'll need to know the name servers to point your domain name to. They usually look something like: NS1. HOSTINGSERVICE.COM and NS2.HOSTINGSERVICE.COM. The name servers tell the Internet where to look for your web site. Your name server settings are updated within your domain name account.

Remember this: Once you have your:
1. Domain name (and access to set your DNS).
2. Web hosting account (to upload your files).
3. Web editing software. (to create and upload files)
you're ready to build and manage your web site.

Chapter 4 (Understanding Search Engines)

The Spider

Just about every major search engine has three main parts. The first is the spider, otherwise called a robot or document locator. The spider visits a web page, reads it, and then follows links to other pages within the site. This is what it means when someone refers to a site being "*spidered*" or "*crawled*." The spider returns to the site on a regular basis, such as every month or so, to look for changes and updates. (If a site is updated often and is well marketed, the spider will return more often, sometimes even every day).

The Index

Everything the spider finds goes into the second basic part of a search engine, the index. The index, sometimes called the database or document corpus, is like a giant library containing a copy of every web page that the spider finds. If a web page is different or appears to have changes, then the site will be re-indexed and this "*database*" is updated with new information.

Sometimes it can take a while for new pages or changes that the spider finds to be added to the index. Thus, a web page may have been "*crawled*" but not yet "*indexed*." Until the new information is indexed, it is not available to those searching with the search engine.

The Algorithm

The third, and most sophisticated part of a search engine is the ranking software (sometimes referred to as the '*algo*' or algorithm). This is the program that sifts through the millions of pages recorded in the index to find matches to a search and rank them in order of what it believes is most relevant.

All search engines have the basic parts described above, but there are major differences in how these parts are tuned. That is why the same search on different search engines often produces different results.

Search Engine Algorithms

Search technology has evolved in many ways within the past few years. The technology involved has transformed from a simple mathematical science to what seems like an artificial intelligence.

Several years ago, the algorithm involved in comprehending a web page consisted of a simple process of examining *meta tags (Chapter 11)* and counting the words on a web page. Today, this process has evolved into a sophisticated comprehension of a web site and everything which surrounds it.

Count, spell, define, measure and more.

A sophisticated search engine like Google, can interpret a web sites overall theme while defining content, checking spelling, calculating relevance, measuring *PageRank (Chapter 8)* (the trust or authority of a page), translating languages, identifying its owner, tracing its geographic origin, and plenty more all within a fraction of a second. In this document we will explore in detail some of the many processes that a search engine uses to comprehend a web site.

A search engine algorithm comes into play after a search engine scans or "*crawls*" a web site to read and comprehend it. Search engine crawlers, also referred to as "*spiders*", scan the entire web through links from one page to another and store a record of web pages for each and every web site on the Internet. This information is stored within a network of computers making up a giant index of data. Search engines then run that data through a computer algorithm and apply something in-tune with a "*score*" for a sites importance, trust, authoritativeness, relevance and quality. Sites which score high are displayed at or near the top of search engines for the keywords related to the web site. The process search engines use to deliver results takes a fraction of a second from the time a search is initiated.

The computer algorithms used by search engines are very complex in nature and change often. Google and other popular search engines like Yahoo and Bing use hundreds of ranking factors in their *algorithms (Chapter 30)* in order to examine the web site itself, the links that point to the web site, historical data for a site, traffic patterns, domain names, social signals and hundreds of other things a computer program has the ability to record and analyze. Over the years it has become increasingly important for search engines to perfect these algorithms due to the tremendous amount of sites on the Internet. Search engines must deliver the best and most relevant results to maintain their reliability, trust and popularity among users.

Today, Google.com is clearly the most accurate and widely used search engine in the world *(Chapter 14 Google Is King)* delivering search engine results to over one billion users (1,000,000,000) per month and generating nearly thirty eight billion dollars ($38,000,000,000.00) per year in revenue. Every search engine in the world has followed suit with similar processes in an attempt to compete with Google and all, for the most part, have failed. The company is highly motivated to keep its underlying search engine processes top secret to remain the leader in search. Through the popularity and use of Google's search results the service virtually creates the winners and losers of the web making or breaking businesses and brands.

Some of the algorithm changes that have rolled out this year alone fundamentally change search as we know it. Results based not only by relevance, but by the popularity and authority of the author and the increasingly powerful characteristics search engines are using from social networks as well as the verification of geographical targets *(Chapter 27 localization)* and other factors are completely changing what we have seen in years gone by. Today, the results displayed are different for each and every user. In March, Google released new privacy terms which indicated they will be using the habits of users to fine tune their results to what Google thinks specific users like, or don't like. User connections or friends on Google+ contribute to a profile of you, who you are and what you do.

Ever since Google Inc. went public in 2004, they have become more and more driven by revenue. Google's primary revenue generator is driven by ads, the pay per click sponsored results seen on web sites and alongside search results; keeping us all in the dark as to why some sites appear and some sites don't, drives ad dollars. So you can bet your bottom dollar they'll keep their results as complicated as possible, as best they can.

Chapter 5 (When Should You Submit?)

Although submitting your site is simple, you do not necessarily need to submit your web site to any search engine. Search engines find your web site through links which point to your pages.

Companies who say they *"submit"* your web site to hundreds or thousands of search engines are either very misinformed or taking advantage by selling you a service in which you do not need.

There are just three major search engines which deliver the majority of all traffic on the web and these search engines are already aggressively seeking your content. If you currently have a web site online, chances are, popular search engines already know about it. If not, you can add your site to Google, Yahoo and Bing for free although there is no guarantee they will accept it. To submit your content visit:

- **Google Webmaster Tools:**
  http://www.google.com/submityourcontent/

- **Bing and Yahoo! Webmaster Tools**
  https://ssl.bing.com/webmaster/SubmitSitePage.aspx

Yahoo and Bing: With the completion of Yahoo's algorithmic transition to Bing (In 2011 Bing became the provider of search results for Yahoo), Yahoo! Search has merged into Bing Webmaster Tools. Webmasters should now be using the Bing Webmaster tools to submit and enhance listings in organic search results for both Bing and Yahoo!

How Most Sites Get Listed

Getting listed in a search engine generally happens naturally. Placing just one link on an individual publicly accessible web page or social network is enough for Google and other search engines to find you. Twitter, Facebook, LinkedIn, etc., are all useful for this purpose. Again, all you need to do is post your web site URL on a social network and search engines will find it. Links to your web site help increase the rankings of your web pages and the more quality links you have pointing to your web site, the better your site will perform in search. Links directly affect the way search engines rank your web pages.

Improving Your Rankings

Having a great site, a good idea or a unique service isn't enough to make it with your Internet business. You need visibility on search engines to matter, period. All businesses are recognizing that online success is found through increasing traffic to their web site.

Search engine optimization *(also called SEO – Chapter 7)* is a complex technical process of adjusting your web site architecture which positions your site higher in the results of search engines when users seek whatever it is they need, at a time when they need it. This is because optimizing your pages helps search engines read and comprehend what's on them.

In advertising, timing is indeed everything, and getting your marketing pitch to a consumer when he or she is actively searching is absolute key. It's the most direct and targeted marketing you'll find.

Chapter 6 (Filing A Reconsideration Request)

Requesting a reconsideration of your site after it has been removed from search engines, or its ranking has decreased, is the only time you should rely on a submission process. If your site isn't appearing in Google search results, or it's performing more poorly than it once did, you can ask Google to reconsider your site. It is very important to ensure your site doesn't violate Google's Webmaster Guidelines before doing so.

The process consists of

- Analyzing your site for violations.
- Fixing or removing instances which cause problems.
- Submitting a detailed request for reconsideration with Google.

It can take just days or several weeks for Google to process these requests.

To find out more visit:
https://www.google.com/webmasters/tools/reconsiderati on

Bing and Yahoo have a similar process available through Bing Webmaster Tools. If your site was detected to serve malware or used spam techniques and was removed from Bing and Yahoo, index penalties can be lifted. Once you have resolved these issues and republished your site, you can request a reconsideration from the Bing support team.

For more on processes specific to Bing / Yahoo visit:
http://onlinehelp.microsoft.com/en-us/bing/hh204494.aspx

Webmaster Guidelines

Read each search engines' guide lines and follow them strictly. This will ensure your site is not penalized for any reason. Having your website penalized by a major search engine like Google, could have an irreversible and quite horrific effect on your marketing efforts.

Webmaster Tools

All major search engines have a free Webmaster service for webmasters. These areas allow webmasters to check indexing status and optimize visibility of their websites.

They have tools that let webmasters submit and check sitemaps, check statistics about how search engine crawlers access a site, generate and check robots.txt files, discover pages that are blocked, list pages that link to the site and analyze more technical aspects as well as help webmasters communicate with search engines.

For Google's Webmaster Tools visit:
https://www.google.com/webmasters/

For Bing's (and Yahoo!) Webmaster Tools visit:
http://www.bing.com/toolbox/webmaster

RECONSIDERATION REQUEST SCENARIO #1

Request Processed Confirmation:

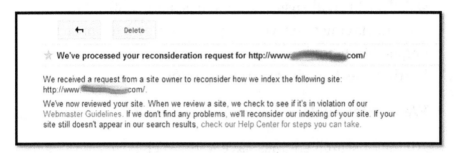

Response (Manual Spam Action Revoked):

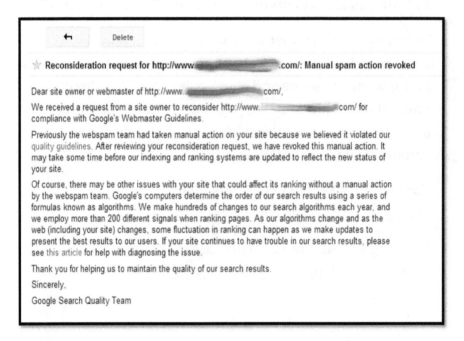

The above example of a reconsideration request indicates that a site was manually penalized by Google and upon resolution and communication (submission response – picture 1) the penalization was removed (action taken notification – picture 2).

RECONSIDERATION REQUEST SCENARIO #2

Initial Request Confirmation:

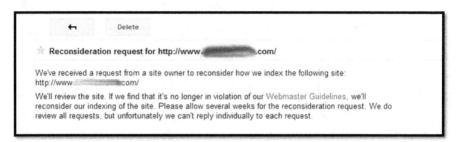

Response (No Manual Spam Actions Taken):

The above is an example of a reconsideration request which indicted that no manual penalization took place and upon communication (submission response – picture 1) the webmaster was notified that no penalization was removed (no action taken notification – picture 2).

Chapter 7 (Search Engine Optimization)

Search engine optimization (SEO) is the process of *'optimizing'* the architectural aspects of a web site for search engines. How a site is designed plays a crucial role in how much organic (*natural*) traffic it will receive from search.

Search engines tend to give 'high rankings' to sites designed with search engine optimization in mind. This is due to the fact that optimized web sites are easier for search engines to understand. They're more predictable. When search engines like Google can comprehend everything on a web site, chances are substantially increased for the site to pop up well. Problem is, not all web sites are designed with search in mind. They're often designed to look good, be *'flashy'*, and incorporate all the bells and whistles initially requested of the designer, but they're often lacking what web site owners need most - and that's the ability to harness TRAFFIC on their own.

When and if search engines cannot properly define your content, products or services, they'll simply resort to different or better sites which they can. With over 8 billion (8,000,000,000) web pages to sift through, search engines like Google have plenty on their plate to serve and don't want to take guesses at what a service is offering - they want to be sure about it. As the saying goes, there are plenty of fish in the sea, so you'll have to shine and stick out to be competitive in search engines - especially today.

So what's the bottom line? Search engine optimized web sites attract more info-hungry visitors from search; having a poorly optimized site can easily cost you natural traffic.

Search engine optimization fundamentals:

- Meta and Page Title Tags (Titles, keywords, description)
- Keyword Written Content (Keyword density and sales)
- Internal Linking Structure (Anchor text, navigation)
- Site Crawl-ability (Spider-ability, site links, etc.)
- Link Building (Your measure of importance/popularity)
- On-Page Optimization (ALT tags, file names, other elements)
- Keyword Research (Making sure you're going after the right terms)
- Sitemaps (Page availability, spider-ability)
- Usability (how users interact with your site)

On-Page Search Engine Optimization Elements

Simply put, "on-page" elements consist of anything which makes up the web site itself. This can consist of content, keywords, images, files, contact forms and any information or architectural aspects of back-end coding (the non-visible elements of what is seen by the naked eye). Something as simple as a structure, shape, layout and colors could play a crucial role.

When someone refers to "*on-page*" changes to a web site, they're generally referring to things that can be changed on a web site to ensure search engines understand and "*index*" a web site in a way which makes the site relevant to what its purpose is. It also means the site has been inspected to ensure there isn't anything on the web site that a) may be counterproductive to the overall goals or b) may contain anything which would appear to a search engine as being possibly "*over-optimized*" (a new characteristic Google is looking for) or even web spam, such as hidden text.

If the intent is to rank well for the keyword "*advertising company*", it is important to ensure that search engines understand that the web site is about that topic specifically. This is done by "*optimizing*" the elements on the web site for that term and ensuring that those terms "*stand-out*" to search engines, while at the same time, doesn't' stand out "*too much*" where it would be considered "over optimized".

If and when search engines correlate a significant relevance to a term on the web site or web page and it's also matched with a high algorithmic score (the site is trusted), the page will appear well within SERPS (search engine results pages) when people search for the term or other terms like it.

Using ALT attributes in your source code

Visually impaired users and most search engines are not always able to distinguish what an image is. Using image alt attributes allows you to help screen readers and search engines understand what an image represents by providing a text equivalent for the object. In other words, alt attributes allow you the opportunity describe the image with text so they have meaning to both search engines and blind users.

```
<img src="http://www.yoursite.com/images/house.gif"
height="140" width="120" alt="House for Sale." />
```

Blind users and search engines can now use the alt attribute to comprehend there is a picture of a "House for Sale" on the page and that the picture is 140 pixels high by 120 pixels wide. Alt tags help keyword relevance when search engines scan your pages.

Using Canonical Tags

Many sites which use programming to create dynamically created URL's have errors or bugs within their systems that cause problems for search engines. When the software is initially developed, it isn't developed with search engines in mind, so although small errors or bugs do not affect the look, feel or use of the software, they cause havoc for search engines when it comes to crawling and identifying pages. Sites which use inconsistent link structures unknowingly cause the exact same content to get indexed under multiple URLs. This creates "Duplicate Content" and pages get penalized for this.

Using a canonical tag tells search engines which URL is the correct version to index. Search engines try to identify the most authoritative URL but adding a canonical tag makes this easier.

Examples of common URLs which may contain the same content hosted on different web addresses are:

- http://www.yoursite.com
- http://yoursite.com
- http://www.yoursite.com/default.asp
- http://yoursite.com/default.asp
- http://yoursite.com/default.asp?affiliate_id=45

Having all of the pages with the same content but different URL's is just plain old confusing for search engines. To address this issue installing the following tag let's search engines know which one they should index:

```
<link rel="canonical" href="http://www.yoursite.com">
```

The tag is placed in between the <head> and </head> tags of your source code. It tells search engines that http://www.yoursite.com is the correct version and is the correct URL to use for both indexing and listing the site in search; all links, PageRank, and authority should be directed to this particular URL structure.

Using the "nofollow" Tag

This attribute should be used to prevent a link from passing link authority. Although they are commonly used on sites with user generated content (like classifieds or forums), Google requests webmasters use the nofollow tag anytime a link is not editorial in nature. This helps Google know if it should or shouldn't pass PageRank to the linked document.

It has also been stated by Google that "nofollow" links do not affect *SERPs (via "anchor text" Chapter 10),* but some webmasters, including myself, still theorize that they do hold some weight, although the official answer from Google is that they do not. I'm personally not buying it though. I do not feel a good enough amount of the web is using the "nofollow" tag appropriately and it simply, in my opinion, does not make sense to avoid following all links with the tag. For instances, Twitter uses them on every single post. Is this to mean that every post on Twitter is not followed? It just doesn't seem practical to ignore all links with the tag.

The code to use "nofollow" on a link appears like:

```
<a rel="nofollow" href="http://www.site.com">anchor
text </a>
```

The nofollow tag can also be used in a robots meta tag to prevent a search engine from counting any outbound links on a page. This code would look like this:

```
<meta name="robots" content="nofollow">
```

Note: More examples of meta tags will be covered in the chapter called "Meta Tags and How To Use Them"

Off-Page Search Engine Optimization Elements

Off-page or "*off-site*" optimization refers to anything that doesn't have a direct effect to the look, feel, or architectural aspect of a web site. In other words, nothing on the site itself is being changed in this process; it's entirely "off-site" marketing. For instance, links pointing from other sites can be "*optimized*" for relevance using appropriate anchor text. Anchor text is the actual text based words in the link itself which point to a web site. Anchor text plays a significant role in search engine rankings and using the appropriate anchor text when linking can be very effective. Social signals, article marketing, press releases and any online references to a site can be considered off-page optimization.

Recently, Google has been quite forthcoming with the fact that they are assigning importance and a measure of value to web sites which maintain a level of brand recognition with users. As it is extremely unlikely that brand value could be optimized on-page, this too can be considered an "*off-site*" optimization process.

The popularity of a web site, how often it is clicked among other results, social signals, web links that point to it, as well as other user behaviors can determine a web sites brand value. This is one of the newer and significant algorithm change search engines are using in addition to their process of web site evaluation.

Search Engine Optimization Guidelines

Search engines release publicly available guidelines about relevance, optimization, as well as over optimization or search engine spam. It is important for web site operators to strictly adhere to these specific *guidelines (Chapter 6)* as those who don't could find themselves in much worse shape than when they started the optimization process to begin with.

Being found on Google and other popular search engines can make or break any business in today's Internet savvy marketplace. Those who understand not just the desired result, but the process involved in making that result possible, as well as maintaining those results over time will reap larger rewards, with less expense. This effectively increases the overall Return On Investment (ROI) for companies that utilize search engine optimization as a business marketing process.

Chapter 8 (Google's Infamous PageRank™)

In 1998 Lawrence Page, now the Chief Executive Officer of Google Inc. began preparing a United States patent to protect a unique and innovative technological process he had created that would determine the value of a web page based upon the hypertext links pointing to it. The patent is titled "Method for Node Ranking in a Linked Database" and has become known by industry insiders as "The PageRank Patent" *(We'll tear into some Patents in Chapter 30)*. This process began the official presentation for "Google", a prototype large-scale search engine which made heavy use of the structure present in hypertext *(links)*.

At the time, most search engines used primitive methods of deciphering pages entirely by the words or text present on the web site and within code created by the designer. This simple and much outdated method returned search results based entirely on keyword matches and the quantity of those keywords on pages being evaluated by search engines.

Eventually this led to webmasters littering their pages with keywords just to pop up when people searched. Page clearly knew that a better method was required in order to deliver search results based on additional factors similar to a reputation based system and one which relied more on references made by others.

What is Google PageRank™ and does it matter?

PageRank™ is the measure of importance developed and patented by Page. PageRank™ is displayed on the Google Toolbar and is a green bar used on many tools and plugins, generally related to the browser of your computer. Many site owners go after PageRank™ as a main focus of link building and use it to discover opportunities for building links to their web site. Years ago, PageRank™ was more important than it is today when it comes to link building. In the past, if a high page rank site (one with many links pointing to it) linked to you, that PageRank™ would transfer to your site.

Today this works a little differently than it did in the past.

PageRank™ is created through links across the web. A web site can have a PageRank™ level of 0 – 10, zero is usually displayed for new web sites or those with very few links pointing to them, and 10 when many sites on the Internet are linking to it. Sites with a rating of 10 are usually huge sites like Yahoo, Google, or those with millions of links like Adobe.com or Apple.com. The basic or general PageRank™ of a typical site is usually around a 3, 4 or 5.

PageRank™ has a significant value to web sites because usually sites with high PageRank™ rank very well in search engines, but this is really only an indication of how many links the site has, so it isn't necessarily the PageRank™ itself, but the links the PageRank™ is created from.

In the past, PageRank™ was the single identifier marketers would hunt for when targeting link building strategies, but today things have changed some as PageRank™ may or may not flow to the target site which is determined by many other factors which did not play into the game years ago.

Today, high PageRank™ sites may not even pass any PageRank™ at all, so those who are going after PageRank™ without looking at other very relevant things like *'theme'* and *'outbound links'* are missing the boat, either partially or entirely. Just because a site has high PageRank™ and you have a link pointing to your site from it, doesn't necessarily mean that PageRank™ will flow through to your site. This is why you really need to evaluate who your linking partners are and where the links pointed at your site are coming from.

In the event you're building links to your site, and you do not know how or when which links count and why, you could easily spend a whole lot of money purchasing ads and links with little return.

At the end of the day the best thing to do is to not get yourself all wrapped up on PageRank™. It clearly isn't the end-all be-all of search engines rankings or site popularity. Yes, sites with high PageRank™ usually indicate powerful, authoritative sites, but many times you will see a lower PageRank™ page out rank a higher PageRank™ page anyway.

The most important thing is that you focus on providing great content, a positive experience for users and to acquire links to your site based more on relevance and theme relation than what the PageRank™ of the page may be. It is important to bring as much traffic as possible to your site from other sites that are relevant to yours. Do that, and a reasonable amount of PageRank™ is sure to follow.

Chapter 9 (How Link Popularity Works)

"In life, reputations are based upon judgment by peers; online it's defined by links." John Colascione

When you understand "link popularity" you can easily understand link building strategies. Link popularity is basically summed up as having a popularity contest between two web sites where the quantifiable value is based on hypertext links. The web site with the most links wins but it isn't the sheer number of links that matters most and this is where it gets complicated.

First, we'll need to understand the basics of link popularity.

A web site with ten (10) links pointing to it is obviously measured to be more *"popular"* (where links are the quantifiable item) than a web site with only one (1) link pointing to it. As such, a web site which has one hundred (100) links pointing to it would obviously be more *"popular"* than a web site with only fifty (50) links pointing to it. This is pretty simple to understand. Basically, the web site with the most links wins, which is the way *it used to be.*

- But what if the links couldn't be counted by number or quantity?
- What if links were counted more on quality, then quantity and then scored based on that?
- What if having 1 link could be better than having 100 links?

Now we start to create an interesting situation. Those who understand this process and that 1 link could be better than

10, 20, or even 100 other links are going to save time, effort and avoid ending off worse than where they started.

Link building (Chapter 10) is important for your site because search engines count the number of links which point to you in order to come up with an idea of your sites' popularity. But search engines look at more than the sheer number of links. They measure how important each link is and whether or not it should be counted to begin with.

Having too many of the wrong links could also damage your site by

1. Pointing too many links which create or dilute the keyword rankings you have now.

2. Pointing too many links with exact anchor text or are irrelevant causing an 'over optimization' penalty or otherwise signal spam attempts.

It is important to acquire the right mix of links in a natural way as great and popular sites will have many different types of links pointing to them.

Chapter 10 (All About Link Building)

As discussed in Chapter 9, linking to your site is important and determines how your site ranks in search engines. Have you ever wondered why certain sites rank where they do? Links which point to web sites are one of the most significant factors when search engines determine how important web sites are in comparison to other sites.

This works on a system similar to *popularity factors discussed in Chapter 9*. Depending on how popular your site is greatly effects how and when people find it in search engines.

In a nutshell, if there are many web sites on the Internet which point to your site using specific "anchor text", your site will begin to rank better for those terms based on the fact that it is often referred to with that exact "anchor text".

For example, if your site was about link building, you want to build links with the actual words *"Link Building"* as the clickable keywords in the link.

"Anchor text" is extremely important to search engines when it comes to placing relevance to a particular web site based on its links. Anchor text tells search engines: *"this is what the web site is about"*. Clearly, the optimal link to your site will contain your main keyword phrase.

Let's say you have a website that sells car insurance online. When you solicit links, and fail to give guidance as to what the link should look like, you will commonly get something along the lines of a company name like "Smith International LTD" as the clickable link text. This is great if you want to be found for only your company name. It is, however, far from the ideal.

The ideal link would be something like "Cheap Car Insurance", whereby only "Cheap Car Insurance" contains the link. If this whole sentence is too long, simply "Car Insurance" or just "Insurance" is preferable.

There is also evidence, although not conclusive, that the title attribute can add a ranking boost. So let's take the example above and show you the html code for it.

```
<a title="Insurance"
href="http://www.smithinternational.com">Car Insurance</a>
```

In the case above, this link will help your site rank for the term "Car Insurance".

If you do not specify the html code to be used upon successfully soliciting a link, you will very likely just end up with the following:

```
<a href="http://www. smithinternational.com">Smith
International LTD</a>
```

Or worse,

```
<a href="http://www. smithinternational.com">
www.smithinternational.com</a>
```

(Note: This is why domains with keywords in them tend to do well. When someone links to you without anchor text, keywords are still included to some extent, even if only in the web address.)

If there were keywords in the domain, even if someone just linked to you with the name of the URL or company, you would still gain a keyword (insurance) in the anchor text.

> *<a href="http://www.smithinsurance.com">Smith Insurance</a>*

Clearly, not specifying the exact text to be used wastes a good link opportunity. In this example above you can also clearly see how having good keywords in your URL can be beneficial when it comes to gaining links – not to mention the relevance the keyword in the URL lends to the site overall.

The solution, therefore, is to provide a webmaster who has agreed to link to you with the exact html code. This has two main advantages: 1) the webmaster will be grateful, as all he/she has to do is copy and paste the code and slap it into his/her site. 2) you also get the text link that does your site the most good.

Not knowing about anchor text and using it properly could cost you the benefit of great rankings. For example, if you built many links pointing to your site, but you did not use keyword driven anchor text and rather used something like "click here", your page would have a good chance at ranking somewhere within the millions of pages which rank for "click here" but that would do you virtually no good.

The trick is ranking well for terms which are important and highly relevant and related to the content and subject matter of your site. This is done through on page optimization, internal and external linking, and other forms of optimization and marketing.

Where to Get Good Links

Submit your site to valuable and popular web directories like Yahoo.com, DMOZ.org and BOTW.org to gain come creditability from authoritative sources. These directories have been around for many years. Submitting and getting listed in DMOZ (The Open Directory Project) is important as the directory is also used by Google to build its own web directory. Unfortunately DMOZ is not maintained as well as it was in the past and getting listed is difficult and/or sometimes even impossible as editors take very long to approve listings, but you should still at least submit.

Deep Linking

A deep link is a link that points somewhere within your website, but not to the home page. Deep links are important for many reasons. Let me give you an example of why a deep link is important.

Say you run a website about auto parts and installation of such. If you have a page about how to install a fuel filter, the file name for the page on your site may be named this: _www.myautoparts.com/install-filter.html_. This page could be a detailed instruction sheet with step by step instructions on how to install a filter. If this page is a good and valuable resource, people will want to link to it. They will probably be linking to you from a page about your target market, auto parts or car repair, both would be excellent inbound links which would point deep into your site.

This would translate to a search engine that there is valuable information to be found on your website, not just on the homepage, but specific pages which are great – and people are linking to them. This is generally a telltale sign of a good web site (a characteristic you want to display).

Let's take another example. The website Adobe.com has hundreds and thousands of links pointing to it because of the tremendous value their software provides the computer industry. Thousands of these links are deep links pointing to the download software pages like this: http://get.adobe.com/reader/

This tells a search engine that not only is the site itself important, but a subfolder on the subdomain within this site is useful and important. Not only that, but in a discussion on *PageRank™ (Chapter 8)* and how it is distributed throughout the entire site, this will deliver much needed PageRank™ to inner pages within your website. PageRank™ will flow deep within the site and then eventually be returned to the homepage (as long as these deep pages all link back to the homepage).

There is an endless amount of good to creating deep links to your website. The better and more useful your content, the more likely you are to create deep links naturally. If your site has no deep links, you should start finding ways to best acquire them. Basically, it is better to have some deep links than to have none. I guess you can think of it like this: If you had a group of 10 men, and only 1 of them had any friends, there is probably only 1 of them worth talking to.

Forget Building links.... Build BIG links.....

If your serious about building a future on the web, you'd better start building some "BIG" links, and what I mean by "BIG" is serious value sites. You're going to need to focus less on how many links you can get, and start focusing on where you can get them from.

Basically the idea of all this stems from the industry and what search engines must do to rank webpages. Almost every webmaster across the net has learned that building inbound links to your website is a major part of search engine optimization. This is resulting in massive amounts of link exchange requests, link schemes, a little littering of the net along with major marketing campaigns targeting web directories and text link advertising.

For search engines to maintain the quality and integrity users have come to expect, especially from search engines like Google, search engines have no choice but to re-create the value assigned to a website and how it is established.

Links from high quality heavy traffic news websites are a very good example of where you would want to acquire a link from. Search engine professionals as well as the creators of the algorithms know that these types of links aren't exactly easy to acquire and are generally based more on merit than marketing.

If you're in a small niche market, you'll want to target top properties in related industries and get links from those sites. You could spend 8 hours buying 200 links, or eight days acquiring 1 real "BIG" link, and be much better off.

People always try to build links wherever they can, but these days, if it takes you 3 months with emails back and forth to acquire 1 very strong relevant link, you'd be better off doing that. Great powerful links based on true effort can reap "huge rewards" for years to come. It's never a wasted effort putting significant time into acquiring a powerful backlink, especially from a state or governmental site.

I've personally made plenty of calls, faxed forms, and mailed written letters for both link opportunities and partnerships which could turn into links. I've never regretted those efforts and probably developed some of my best inbound links that way. It makes a big difference.

Methods of Developing Links

There are many methods of developing backlinks. When starting a link building campaign, one of the first things people often do is to analyze what their competitors are doing. Looking at where your competitors are getting links is one of the easiest ways to identify new link opportunities for your own site. In addition to getting links from the same sources as your competitors, you should also look at the types of sites are already linking to you, and see how you can manage to get more links on similar type sites. Just copying your competitors' links will leave you constantly behind them, so it is important to think outside of the box and use the link strategies outlined below to outrank them.

Contextual Links

One of the best ways to build links for Search Engine Optimization purposes is to obtain contextual links that are editorial in nature. Contextual links refer to links within the content of the page. These kinds of links are effective for *Search Engine Optimization (Chapter 7)* because they're natural to search engines. By getting a contextual link on a high PR page which also has a low number of outbound links to external sites ensures that your link will be assigned most of the authority the page has to offer since the measure of value isn't spread thin between all the links on that page. Each time a link is placed on a page, a small percentage of link value diminishes for other links on the page.

Article Marketing

You can also develop good long lasting backlinks through article marketing. Article marketing is a great way in which to demonstrate expertise in your field. Quality articles are submitted to article databases or to industry web sites. You gain exposure to your web site through backlinks that are contained within the text of the article and also in the author information box (sometimes called the boilerplate) associated with the article. Article marketing can help your site gain links because depending on the quality of the article, it could be syndicated, copied and/or reused on other sites, and when your links are also included, this just means additional links and references to your site from niche material.

Reciprocal Links

Another popular method is (or was) to develop reciprocal links. These are links in which your link is listed on another web site and, in exchange, you have a link to that web site on yours. This has become much less popular these days from abuse, but it still does work very well in situations where the linking partners are covering very related topics. Reciprocal links still work for rankings and traffic if the theme related between the sites are similar. If a golf site trades links with another golf site, you'll still see a benefit of both rankings and traffic with this exchange. It's the unrelated reciprocal links that don't work.

Why reciprocal links don't work:

Reciprocal links are not classified the same as normal links. A reciprocal link is when a website links to another website only to return the favor (link exchange).

Example: WEBSITE A links to WEBSITE B, and then to return the favor WEBSITE B links to WEBSITE A.

That is considered a reciprocal link exchange. This will get you nowhere in the long run if the two sites have nothing to do with each other. Search engines know that this is a link exchange, tactic to attempt to boost traffic and link popularity. They've become wise to this and diminish the value of reciprocal links between unrelated sites.

Quality Link:

- WEBSITE A has an article about "widgets" and links to WEBSITE B (widgets.com) which details even more about widgets.
- WEBSITE B (widgets.com) doesn't link back.
- WEBSITE A's link to WEBSITE B is a quality outbound link.
- WEBSITE B's link from WEBSITE A is a quality inbound link.

Search engines love quality links. They will send you to the information that it thinks you're looking for, and just in case it's not enough, the search engine knows that there is a quality link there that will provide you with more.

Note: Major search engines are likely not giving value to websites that are linked to from pages named /links.asp, /links.php, /links.html or /links.htm - This should be taken into consideration when swapping links with other webmasters.

IP addresses and Links

An IP address is the location of a computer or web server on the Internet. It is usually 4 sets of digits, known as octets. The third octet is called the C-Class IP address.

This example of an IP address: 214.95.*164*.91

164 is the C-Class IP address.

The purpose of a domain name is simply to map a web site name to an IP address. It's a whole lot easier to remember mywebsite.com instead of 214.95.164.91 don't you think? Every web site is hosted on an IP address like the example above. Some webmasters or marketing companies set up multiple websites with similar content and link them together to achieve higher-rankings in the search engines. Such sites are known as 'Mirror Sites'.

If you're setting up multiple websites using the same web hosting provider, chances are your websites will be on the same IP address or at least the **same C-class IP address**. This basically means that one site will be here 214.95.164.91 and one site will be here 214.95.164.92, but both reside on the same block which is 214.95.164 (the first three octets) as it indicates the same owner is in control of that hosting space. It is important not to have several sites linking to each other that reside on the same C-Class IP address. This is an important factor for anyone concentrating on text link marketing, or paying someone to do so. You want to avoid having too many links pointing at your site from the same IP address or the same IP block because it could be seen as an attempt to inflate PageRank™.

There are hosting companies that offer "SEO Hosting" which offer multiple C-Class IP's and offer separate blocks to the same client, but Google and other search engines are getting hip to these type of tactics and it just isn't worth getting involved trying to game (*get over on*) Google because chances are they'll identify it with other means.

Comments and Forums

Another method of developing backlinks is through forum or blog comments. Those who do this well maintain a viable '*purpose*' for the comment by generating useful and/or valuable discussion within a community of contributors. Small relevant comments are left on forums or blogs which are related to the service or product being marketed. These comments contain a backlink to your web site, most often in the signature of the comment or within the content of the message. If you do not plan to leave valuable information in your comment or post, I recommend avoiding this tactic.

Web 2.0 Social Links (Becoming Critical)

Social media marketing is the newest and most innovative method of developing backlinks. With the advent of Twitter, Facebook and other social media outlets, it is possible to create literally thousands of backlinks from these sites. When you post a Tweet or a message on your Facebook wall, the message will not only go out to your followers, but also be posted on the front page or wall of the social media site. Followers who find your post interesting or think their own followers would be interested then forward or 'like' your post, creating even more opportunities for backlinks. Web 2.0 links are a good starting point for link building. When unique content related to your niche is created and submitted to web 2.0 properties around the web, you get highly relevant backlinks to your web page.

For those who are unaware, web 2.0 sites basically refer to a new generation of sites that allow users to interact and collaborate with each other in a social dialogue as creators of user generated content share the link. Prior to web 2.0 most web sites were static (didn't interact with users). An important consideration when creating content for web 2.0 sites is how well the pages rank in Google. If you can get web 2.0 articles to rank well in Google, which is very possible when you write great content and promote that content, not only are you building relevant links to your site to help with SEO, but you can get targeted traffic to your web 2.0 properties from real people interested in discussion. Social media is a powerful way to generate genuine "social buzz" for your brand.

Blogroll Links

These kinds of links ensure your link is on the homepage, the page which usually holds the highest authority on a site. Ideally you want to get contextual links and homepage links using the strategies discussed above but blogroll links are very popular as well. The only negative with blogroll links are that they are usually site wide which means they appear on every single page of a web site, appearing in sidebar. These site wide links have been said to be counted only as one (1) link, regardless that they appear on many pages. They are given one (1) editorial vote by search engines and usually do not appear within surrounding text or relevant context (which is usually better). If you do target quality relevant blogs, I recommend avoiding this too.

Backlinks and links in general are one of the cornerstone strategies of improving search engine rankings through SEO activities. Any effective internet marketing strategy should include the development of links as one of the key elements to obtaining excellent search engine rankings.

Additionally, something to be considered in your link building effort is *"trust"*. Google deciphers which links should pass importance and/or PageRank™ and which should not. The entire idea of trust rank is built on the fact that some sites should be considered *"trusted"* sites and will add value to your pages when they include links to you.

A good example of what would be a trusted site, would be www.yahoo.com, www.dmoz.org, www.suntimes.com, www.cnn.com, www.foxnews.com, www.botw.org, etc.

These types of major sites are very established, which should ,without question, qualify for some level of Google's *"Trust Rank"* algorithm weight. So having a link on *"trusted sites"* could increase your search engine rankings and PageRank™ considerably.

Note: Chapters 22 ("Reputation Management") and 23 ("Content Marketing") have additional suggestions for generating links.

Chapter 11 (Meta Tags & How To Use Them)

Meta tags are strings of HTML code in web sites that give information about the web site they are installed on. They describe it using tags with keywords. Primarily, they are used to tell search engine crawlers what the web site is about, so that it can be included in relevant search results. Meta tags are found in between the<Head> and </Head> tags in your sites source code (HTML).

To correctly use meta tags, ensure that they are relevant to the page content. Using irrelevant, empty, missing, or incorrectly written tags could be counterproductive. Be sure to include the same keywords in your meta data which appear within your content or any page header tags (H1, H2, H3), particularly your primary keyword or key phrase should be in your title and description tags. Using meta tags properly and ethically is important and play a key role in how your site is listed in search engine results pages.

```
<html xmlns="http://www.w3.org/1999/xhtml"><head>
<meta http-equiv="Content-Type" content="text/html; charset=utf-8" />
<title><?php echo $title; ?> (This tag dynamically generates our keyword driven page title)</title>
<meta name="Description" content="<?php echo $metadesc; ?>(This tag dynamically generates a related
meta description dependant on which page is being viewed)">
<meta name="Keywords" content="<?php echo $metakw; ?>(This tag dynamically generates related
keywords dependant on which page is being viewed)">
<meta name="verify-v1" content="6Xjp+kVOhMKD7EXt5c3yeqO7qkSsdsdsdwFwdVnpBHo15gHikPn0=" />
```

The above image is of meta tags (small snippets of code which help describe your site to search engines). Changes to these can and do make a difference to the ranking results of your pages.

The keywords tag has become less important these days as some search engines ignore it, but I still recommend using it. The description tag, which the major search engines still use acts as the text shown below your link in search results.

This description is the first glimpse internet surfers get of your content, so it should tell them immediately what the content is about and contain relevant keywords. From time to time Google will ignore your description tag and use its own description it feels is more relevant. It then displays its own preview of text along with your link, but it still uses the description tag when evaluating your site.

Should you choose to employ description meta tags, try to keep the description below 200 plain text characters. This will make sure that your description fits within the specified length parameters shown on search engine results pages. If it doesn't, it will show only part of your description, which may limit how much information they get to see before they click.

Another attribute that you should use with meta tags (in the event you don't want a page crawled) is the "robots" attribute. Certain values used within the robots tag will tell a search engine crawlers not to index a page, not to crawl it, or not to archive it. This can be useful if your web site includes restricted content or archives you don't want included in search engine results.

Here's the basic layout of meta tags and what they do:

```
<META NAME="TITLE" CONTENT="This is usually the
bold clickable link in search engines and what appears at
the top of browsers.">
<META NAME="DESCRIPTION" CONTENT="This is
where a description of your site goes. Put vital keywords
here but stay under 1000 characters.">
```

<META NAME="KEYWORDS" CONTENT="This, is, where, you, list, all, of, the, keywords, that, pertain, to, your, site, Make, sure, you, put, a, comma, after, each, keyword, and, do, not, repeat, any, keywords, Use, plurals, and, conjunctions, here, and, on, your, pages">

<META NAME="robots" CONTENT="noindex">Google will retrieve the document, but it will not index the document.

<META NAME="robots" CONTENT="nofollow">Google will not follow any links that are present on the page to other documents.

<META NAME="robots" CONTENT="noindex,nofollow"> Google will not index the document or follow any links that are present on the page to other documents.

<META NAME="robots" CONTENT="noarchive"> Google maintains a cache of all the documents that it fetches, to permit its users to access the content that is indexed (in the event that the original host of the content is inaccessible, or the content has changed). If you do not wish Google to archive a document from your site, you can place this tag in the head of the document, and Google will not provide an archive copy for the document.

<META NAME="robots" CONTENT="noindex,nofollow,noarchive"> Google will not index the document or follow any links that are present on the page to other documents. Google will not maintain a cache of all the documents that it fetches, or permit users to access the content that it indexed (in the event that the original host of the content is inaccessible, or the content has changed). If you do not wish Google to archive a document from your site, you can place this tag in the head of the document, and Google will not provide an archive copy for the document.

** META TAGS BELOW HERE DON'T REALLY SEEM TO MAKE ANY DIFFERENCE **

<META NAME="OWNER" CONTENT="Put your email address in this spot.">

<META NAME="AUTHOR" CONTENT="Put your name or company name here.">

<META HTTP-EQUIV="EXPIRES" CONTENT=""> (Leave this blank to tell the spider not to remove your listing after x amount of time.)

<META HTTP-EQUIV="CHARSET" CONTENT="ISO-8859-1"> (This one is not needed and can be removed.)

<META HTTP-EQUIV="CONTENT-LANGUAGE" CONTENT="English"> (Tells the spider what language your site is. Google is pretty good at figuring this out.)

<META HTTP-EQUIV="VW96.OBJECT TYPE" CONTENT="Document"> (You have many choices here, but the default is document.)

<META NAME="RATING" CONTENT="General"> (This is to rate your site if you have adult or PG content. Meant to assist parental settings and safe-search)

<META NAME="ROBOTS" CONTENT="index, follow"> (This tells the spider to follow links on your site and list other pages. They do this anyway without it.)

<META NAME="REVISIT-AFTER" CONTENT="4 weeks"> (This tells the spider to re-visit your site in x amount of time. Google will create its own schedule regardless.)

<META NAME="robots" CONTENT="nofollow"> Google will not follow any links that are present on the page to other documents.

Meta tags may seem obsolete, but they still have the ability to bring swift and positive change when employed correctly as part of any SEO strategy. The key is using them properly, honestly, and with good attributes.

The Keywords Tag <META NAME="KEYWORDS" CONTENT=" "> *(Keyword Length: 200 to 250 characters)*

This tag is important for some but not all search engines. The most popular and powerful search engines actually skip right over this tag since it is usually abused and *"stuffed"* with inappropriate keywords. Again, I recommend you use it anyway. Many search engines still use it. I believe it is still used to decipher your site and authors intentions to be accurate and/or well designed and described. When listing keywords in your meta keywords tag, be sure that you use only keywords that are actually in your sites body text. Do not put a keyword in you meta tag if the keyword is not visible or tightly related to the webpage.

The Descriptions Tag <META NAME="DESCRIPTION" CONTENT=""> *(150 to 200 characters)*

One thing that's very important to note is that a snippet displayed in search results is determined by the search term. In other words, if you search for your company's name, you'll get a different description than what you would get if you search for a keyword phrase that is relevant for your sites content. Generally, Google pulls the description from areas of the page that surround the usage of that keyword phrase.

Since most people aren't going to be searching for the name of your business, don't try to optimize your Google snippet description based on a search for your company name. Instead, search for the most important keyword phrase for each important page of your site, and then make changes accordingly. It's a good practice to write an accurate and keyword rich meta description which describes the content on the page which will be seen first when the page loads.

The Title Tag <META NAME="TITLE" CONTENT="">
(Title Length - 60 to 70 characters)

This tag usually determines the clickable link to your site displayed in search results. Google sometimes creates its own title tag for your site based on links to your site or other factors, so if this changes depending on the keywords searched or links to your site, Google could be automatically changing it and disregarding your chosen title tag.

Remember that the title and link of your page in search engines is crucial when it comes to increasing click through rates to your site.

Chapter 12 (Example of Algorithm Hypothesis)

It has been said that search engines like Google use hundreds if not thousands of characteristics about web sites they crawl, index and list. The below is an example of how these search engines may prioritize the things they find in order to score documents based on what is determined to be the pages value attributes.

- 30% Link Popularity - Links from other sites - Link and surrounding text analysis - Link IP analysis – Link provider authority
- 15% Title <TITLE>Keyword Phrase - The Keyword Use</TITLE>
- 10% Site Seniority - Domain Name Age and Internet Archive Data Analysis
- 8% Heading Text - <H1>Keyword Phrase</H1> - <H2>Secondary Keyword Phrase</H2> (may vary with .css style usage)
- 8% Body Text - Actual content on page containing important keywords.
- 7% Images - ALT text (hover over text) - File name, how images are viewed.
- 5% URL & File - http://www.keyword.com/keyword.html
- 5% Social Signals: Twitter, Facebook, Google+ social interaction/mentions
- 5% On-Page Link Analysis - Link URL and file names - Link title & text (if text link – the anchor text and destination page) - Link ALT text (if image link).
- 5% Frequency of change to the document; How often the content changes.
- 2% Meta Description Tag and first 2 words in Keywords Tag.

Total Algorithm Score: 100%

The above is just an example of how an algorithm will go through a site and score different items in sort of a checklist of criteria for things to evaluate in order to come up with an overall score for the document (web page).

Google admits: "Relevancy is determined by over 200 factors, one of which is the PageRank for a given page. PageRank is the measure of the importance of a page based on the incoming links from other pages. In simple terms, each link to a page on your site from another site adds to your site's PageRank. Not all links are equal: Google works hard to improve the user experience by identifying spam links and other practices that negatively impact search results. The best types of links are those that are given based on the quality of your content".

Chapter 13 (Why HTML Pages Can Be Better)

HTML (Hypertext Markup Language) is a standardized language of computer code, imbedded in the source behind all web documents, containing the textual content, images, links to other documents, and formatting instructions for display by your browser (the screen). When you view a web page, you are looking at the product of this code working behind the scenes in conjunction with your web browser (Internet Explorer, Google Chrome, Firefox, Safari, etc.). Browsers are programmed to interpret HTML for displaying the visual elements of web sites.

HTML is almost always generated by a human. PHP, ASP, and other scripting languages are a form of HTML, but are generated on the server side and can be created on the fly by a request to a database. A website created and written in a programming language can be set up to literally run by itself, and search engines know this, so it helps them to try and define if a page is being updated manually or automatically. Since a search engine values updated, and fresh content, they check for modifications to web documents in order to see how fresh the information is.

If a search engine finds a page written in HTML which is modified and updated every day, then it's pretty safe to assume that there is an actual human behind this site updating the site frequently (when they can tell the difference). If a search engine finds a page written in some form of programming language updated every day, it needs to be analyzed with stricter guidelines to evaluate whether this was a server side modification to the file, or if there was actually new content generated by a user. This is not always easy for them to determine, but they try. I've seen webmasters try to manipulate this by making their page change a tiny number on the bottom of the page which changes each time the page loads – and not a hit counter.

Search engines look very closely at the *'significance of change'*, the amount of change that took place and whether or not the change should update the value of the page. For instance, if actual content was changed, or a simple auto generated date and time stamped on the page was modified – and was it done automatically by the database, or was it actually modified manually.

Let's get into an example of how the 'significance of change' might be measured and in what cases it would matter.

We will use a Classifieds site for the example.

1. Site A has small miniscule daily updates.
2. Site B has more significant daily updates.

Site A runs a classified ad for 90 days. The database is programmed to run an classified ad for a vehicle with a duration of 90 days and in the event that it does not sell, the program should reset the sale for another 90 days. In this example we will use a "Blue 1955 Model T Ford".

Every time the search engine goes to site A it can tell that there is a "Blue 1955 Model T Ford" listed for sale and that the page is different because the length of time left on the item listed is different. The time and date of the classifieds expire time is generated by the database, so the page is different every time the engine visits, but that really isn't a valuable or *"significant difference"*.

Site B runs a classified ad for 90 days. Every time the search engine goes to site B it can tell that there is a "Blue 1955 Model T Ford" listed for sale and that the page is different because there has been modifications made (let's say they added pictures) in addition to the date change. This is a *"more significant"* change to the page. Not just the date and time left on the listing is different, but there are new pictures. Something of substance has changed, and appears to have been done manually.

Let's examine "the significance" difference in results.

165 days later someone finally queries the engine for a "Blue 1955 Model T Ford". Which site should the search engine return to the end user searching for a "Blue 1955 Model T Ford"? The site which updated it's date and time dynamically each day? Or the site that had a substantial addition manually done (the pictures)?

1. Site A has the item, recent change (date).
2. Site B has the item, recent change (date and photos).

The search engine, when faced with this choice, will usually prefer the more significant change. Plus, the site with only the automated change could easily not be aware that the "1955 Model T Ford" has been sold and is simply, as programmed to do, resetting the ad and running the sale over and over again every 90 days. Site B saw a 'substantial change' to the listing details and likely updated by a human, which is generally more reliable. Site B would be more likely to get the visitor.

Search engines prefer substantial change and human involvement when ranking web pages.

Rewriting URL's

There are instances where HTML can be generated automatically through rule-based rewriting engines (based on a regular-expression parser) to rewrite URLs on the fly. This is called a MOD-REWRITE. It supports an unlimited number of rules and an unlimited number of attached rule conditions for each rule to provide a flexible and powerful URL manipulation mechanism. The URL manipulations can depend on various tests, for instance server variables, environment variables, HTTP headers, time stamps and even external database lookups in various formats can be used to achieve a keyword matching URL.

There are many reasons people like to rewrite URL's with mod rewrite. For one, you can re-write a URL from **"yoursite.com/listing.php?id=28273"** to a better more keyword rich URL like **"yoursite.com/listing/1955-Model-T Ford.html"** which will work a whole lot better in search engines when some searches for a "1955 Model T Ford".

If you're presented with an opportunity to rewrite your URL's with mod re-write, you should take the opportunity to do so. Having keyword rich URL's help search engines define the keyword relevance of the page.

Security of HTML Pages

HTML pages (those without mod rewrite) are also much more secure from hackers. Generally, a site with only .html or .htm file extensions have no programming involved with their functioning and have no database to be managed (and protected). These HTML web sites are much less vulnerable to hacking, SQL injections and other manipulative tactics.

Chapter 14 (Google Is King)

Here are some quick facts on Google's industry position:

- Google is now widely recognized as the world's largest and most sophisticated search engine. An easy-to-use free service that returns relevant results in a fraction of a second.
- Google indexes more than 880 million (880,000,000) images.
- Google receives over 1 billion (1,000,000,000) searches per day.
- Google searches more than 8 billion (8,000,000,000) web pages.
- Google attracts over 1 billion (1,000,000,000) unique visitors per month and is the web's most visited website.
- Google offers its results in 135+ languages and about 70 percent of its traffic comes from outside the U.S.
- Google has 32,467 employees with thousands of PhDs on staff.
- Google reported record revenues of thirty eight billion ($38,000,000,000.00) for the year ending December 31st 2011.
- Most people start their day out on the web by going to Google.
- Google provides email (Gmail) to 350 million (350,000,000) users.
- Google owns the 3rd visited site on the Internet, YouTube.
- Google changes its search algorithm up to 500-600 times per year.

- The word "Google" is now a verb and is defined as" *verb* (used with object) to search the Internet for information about (a person, topic, etc.): We "googled" the new applicant to check her background. *verb* (used without object) to use a search engine such as Google to find information, a Web site address, etc., on the Internet.
- As of March 2012, Google's own web browser "Chrome" became the world's top internet browser.
- Google provides search services to some of the Web's most popular sites, including Amazon, AOL, AT&T, EarthLink and the New York Times.

It seems clear that the aggressive marketer should focus most of his or her attention on Google.

Chapter 15 (Using a Robots.txt File)

A robots file is a simple text (txt) file which is checked before a search engine crawls a website. This file is how you disallow certain documents or directories from getting crawled and/or indexed. If your site doesn't have one, it shouldn't matter too much, but a well-designed and sophisticated site should.

Generally, a robots file is only important if you wish to restrict certain areas of your site from crawlers and label them *"off limits"*. If a search engine requests robots.txt and it isn't there - it will crawl and index the entire site by default.

NOT having a robots file will tell search engines one of two things.

1) The webmaster behind the site is unaware of the files usage and purpose, or,

2) The site owner doesn't care much about robots, what they do or how often they visit.

As you can see, it's importance and usage varies greatly depending on what type of message your trying to relay to search engine crawlers. Generally I recommend using a robots.txt file either way as it is one of few communication channels that are available between a site and search engines.

The "robots.txt" file is also the first place to check when trying to discover exactly what a site wants hidden from search engines. Again, You do not need to have a robots file for your web site, but I recommend having one anyway.

How And Where to Install It

Place the robots.txt file in your root directory (main folder) of your web site. A robots.txt file is a simple notepad (text) document renamed robots.txt.

Most of the time, by default, your Windows computer is not configured to display file names on your desktop which can make changing the file type seem tricky to figure out.

To show file name extensions on Windows

1) Open Folder Options by clicking the Start button
2) Clicking Control Panel
3) Clicking Folder Options
4) Click the View tab, and then, do the following:

To display file extensions, clear the Hide extensions for known file types check box, and then click OK. You will now be able to see and edit file extensions.

Robots.txt Examples

To exclude all search engine robots from your entire site.

> User-agent: *
> Disallow: /

This means user agent = all, disallow = everything.

To allow all robots complete access to your entire site.

> User-agent: *
> Disallow:

This means user agent = all, disallow = nothing.

To exclude all robots from only certain areas of your site.

```
User-agent: *
Disallow: /admin/
Disallow: /documents/
```

This means user agent = all, disallow = the admin and documents folders.

To exclude only a single specific robot

```
User-agent: Google
Disallow: /

User-agent: *
Disallow:
```

This means if the user agent = Google, disallow = the entire site – otherwise if the user agent = anyone else, disallow = nothing

Note: There are a great number of ways to utilize these robots commands including different scenarios where you may want to block only certain robots, to certain areas under only certain circumstances, but these are just some of the main ones your likely to encounter, see in use or decide to use on your web site.

Chapter 16 (Relocating JavaScript)

JavaScript can sometimes take up valuable space in your HTML and may be better off placed elsewhere in an external file. Some search engines are known to index the first 100k of content in a web document. Others are known to give more credit to content placed higher in your HTML (*source code*) and there could be an issue if your JavaScript source code is very large and takes up lots of space in your web document. In this case instead of having a search engine attempt to index a very large document with extensive JavaScript's you would be much better off just placing the entire JavaScript in a separate file called /javascript.js and in the HTML of your web document you'll simply have a string like this:

```
<script
src="http://www.yourwebsite.com/javascript.js"></scrip
t>
```

Relocating JavaScript can save valuable space in your HTML especially if your best content is high on the page but there is large JavaScript's in the header area or anywhere before the <BODY> tags or where the content begins.

Search engines have been said to assign more weight to "*top*" content or readable text that is higher on the page and less weight to content that is lower. This would make sense since you would assume that higher text is read first and lower text may never be seen.

Search engines like Google have improved greatly on how they determine where content or images are actual positioned on a web page after it is loaded in the browser, but it is still advisable to decrease the amount of source code taken up with very large JavaScript's just in case.

Note: One of the reasons search engines have improved the way they handle and decipher this is due to something called CSS Positioning, properties which allow you to position an element anywhere you want on a page despite where it appears in the source code (HTML). Elements can be positioned using the top, bottom, left, and right properties. It can also place an element behind another, and/or specify what should happen when an element's content is too big. Because of this, search engines could not rely on the position of the source code to determine where an element is actually situated on the page, so they must actually view it in a browser like a person to determine actual positions of elements on a page.

Using the process of elimination, it's a whole lot easier to just relocate this code than give it much thought or worry about it. So I recommend leaving small JavaScript's there but relocating very large JavaScript's to an external JavaScript file.

This is very easy to do for sites which contain just a script or two. Just keep in mind that some individual script require their own file, so you if you have a lot of JavaScript's, you could wind up with many JavaScript files, one for each script, but this will be much better than having all those scripts in the actual HTML document.

Chapter 17 (Does W3C Validation Matter?)

I hear this question all too often, and it seems a lot of people spend a lot of time worrying about it, so we'll cover it here for those interested.

The World Wide Web Consortium (W3C) is an international community where Member organizations, a full-time staff, and the public work together to develop Web standards. Led by inventor Tim Berners-Lee and CEO Jeffrey Jaffe, W3C's mission is to lead the Web to its full potential.

Website validation via W3C standards is used to determine a proper coded page from a page that uses invalid coding techniques to the particular version of code being used according to the W3C. In other words, if your using a code from a different version of HTML then described in your DOC TYPE (defined in the top of your HTML document), then you're displaying invalid code (a non-validated page).

Although a browser displays your HTML correctly (most browsers interpret code errors fine) according to the W3C standard, your coding isn't valid.

Currently there are hundreds of thousands of major websites that ARE listed well in search results that do not validate according to the W3C. Examples are major sites like EBay.com, which does not validate and hasn't validated for years. Another major site that does not validate is Yahoo.com. I'd say the majority of popular sites online do not validate according to the W3C standards.

Search engines love valuable information. Valuable information is valuable no matter how you look at it. A search engine will not sacrifice returning information solely based on W3C validation.

Would a search engine return a site that does validate over one that does not? I doubt it very much.

Furthermore, widely known Google engineer Matt Cutts has stated it doesn't matter much in a Webmaster video where a user sent in this exact question and he answered it. I also haven't noticed any signs that it makes any difference at all in my own personal experience and it just didn't seem to matter in every case I've checked it, so I am not sure why it has been such a significant question for so many webmasters over the years, but I do admit that I remember thinking it might play some sort of a role myself years ago.

So, does a strong website marketing plan include making sure your pages validate? I'd have to say no – it doesn't.

If you have a choice (for instance your designer asks you) to have your pages validate or not, I would recommend getting them to validate if you can, just for the heck of it, but if you have any trouble at all, I wouldn't lose any sleep over it as you're very unlikely to suffer any consequences. It's been meaningless to me personally over the years and I don't even know many sites that do validate.

Chapter 18 (Social Media "Algorithmically Speaking")

Why do I need a Twitter or Facebook page? Who cares about that stuff anyway? I just want to rank higher, isn't link building enough?

Well, do you want the honest answer? No it isn't – Not necessarily anymore.... If you want to be even better and rank higher than your competitors it's a good idea to make sure you're covering every base and doing what they might not know about yet. If your competitors are already doing it, then do it better.

FOX® News, CNN®, Coca Cola®, McDonald's®, Disney®, Toyota®, Nike® – these are just some of the world's largest brands which are right now using social media – Yes, they have Twitter.com and Facebook.com accounts – And there is good reason:

Because it works!

Having a social media presence is a lot like having a web site. It is a whole lot better HAVING one than NOT having one.... Sure, you'll still do some business without it here and there, but you'll do a whole lot more if it is easier to find you.

Will it actually increase my sales or leads?

Although it's value for this discussion is how it effects a site algorithmically, well run social media activity can indeed result in direct business (but you must understand that the more genuine interaction with the community, the better results you will see in this area). Here is how:

Have you ever had to see something over and over again until you actually bought it? Heard it on the radio time and time again until you really listened to the commercial and figured out what it was about? Maybe it wasn't the right time, you were busy, you didn't need it at the moment, the mood wasn't right, or you just didn't have any money in your pocket. But then, there it is again…. You know you've heard or seen it before. "I'm going to buy it now".

It's about repetition and staying connected.

Repetition is an important part of advertising. It is through repetition that you establish your credibility, establish brand familiarity, become the first thought when a need for your type of product or service arises, etc. Did you know that scientific research has shown through studies that a person must see your product NINE times before they will be inclined to buy it?

Twitter example:

"There he is…. There is that weird guy Tweeting again… I have some extra time now, let me see what he is all about – Let me see his web site link…" – *BAM, a visit to the web site and a signup.*

This actually does happen. A person sees you and follows you on Twitter (a connection is formed), and then a week later, it happens to be a better time, they see you again, take a closer look, and now they're a customer. Coincidence? I think not:

Social Media Matters

But it isn't just about the laws of repetition. Search engines like Google, Yahoo and Bing have already clearly admitted publically that they do in fact take *"social signals"* into consideration when ranking web pages – and this practice will continue to grow.

Link building has been the core measure of popularity for the last few years, but with an ever-changing complex web of information to sift through, search engines need more than just links, and social signals are filling that void, giving them the extra data they need, when the amount of links you have pointing to you just isn't enough.

Having your products and services discussed, visible, and index-able within social content (social circles), scores extra *"points"* on your behalf…

No one knows exactly how many hundreds or thousands of criteria Google is scoring, but what is known, is that social signals are indeed on the list – and today, likely somewhere near the top.

Now don't get me wrong. Search engines look at a lot more than just this. They look at the number of links that point to your site, the "value" of those links, the value of the linking sites' links (can they trust even those links?), the time people spend on your site, your content, your "authority" (dominance in your niche), your domain name, your sites speed (how fast your site runs), your site architecture, its programming, your sites location, etc. etc. etc.

A social presence could easily be the difference between the characteristics between YOU and your competitor. A search engines fundamental *JOB* is to seek out, find, and evaluate the characteristics of your web site, and decide whether or not they should deliver your material verses someone else's when content matches a search. They must find the overall *BEST* result. They do this by measuring, not only your site, but any evidence it can find on a sites overall importance – "*its value*" – "*your value*" on the web overall, as well as how "*fresh*" "*current*", and "*up-to-date*" your information might be verses your competitor.

Does a site or brand have a social circle presence or not? Just imagine if *YOU* were a search engine and you had to go out and score millions of web pages and rank them based on "*importance*". What would be your opinion of things which were talked about a lot verses things that aren't even mentioned?

Search engines take advantage of similar concepts and use social signals to see what people are "*buzzing*" about. The more something is linked to, tweeted, liked, commented on, shared, etc., the more important it is expected to be.

Ask yourself this:

If you were the owner of a product or service, and no one ever even mentioned it, or the potential for needing it, would you really think it was all that important?

And now, more than ever, Google is trying to associate web pages with people. This is precisely what Google+, the social network, is all about. Knowing about you, what you like, what others like, and who is a '*contributor*' to web sites and web pages. It's not just about serving ads, it's knowing you. It's about search, and it's about understanding You; what you might like verses what someone else might like, and Google is using these social signals to personalize search.

Chapter 19 (Google's Panda: February 2011)

Google changes its search engine often and has been for years, but many changes go unnoticed. The big changes - the ones that really effect a broad range of searches are usually the ones that are named and studied most.

Specifically, Google "Panda", as of the writing of this book, was the most recent significant change to the Google search results and ranking algorithm a long time. It was first released in February 2011. A large part of Panda was about *"cleaning up the web"* and finding out *"what's real"* and *"what's not"*.

Users were getting tired of sifting through garbage in the results and search engines were getting tired of serving it. As search itself becomes more and more competitive, users have increased choices, advertisers and eyeballs become more valuable, and it becomes a search engines key focus and responsibility to deliver the best quality results, in every search, with little to no room for error.

The keyword and focal point to remember for future success is *"Brands"*. Google has been talking about this for a long time now and it is finally becoming a significant part of the algorithm. (On October 13, 2008, Google owner and then Chief Executive Officer Eric Schmidt (now executive chairman) was quoted in an article by CNet.com (CBS Interactive) titled "Brands to clean up Internet Cesspool". The article discussed which sites should be trusted and displayed high in the results and which shouldn't. Brands were indeed the answer.

Most SEO's and experienced marketers have already noticed that 'content' has been specifically targeted, 'domain names' have been specifically targeted, and strong brands are seeing the most benefit from Panda.

It will be increasingly important to remain focused on the types of signals which indicate brand value. Of course, architectural aspects of a site will still play a role, as well as 'links' which will as well, play a very important role, but the types of links may get even more particular.

For instance, links from places which identify and associate a web site with a real "business" may count more.

- Does this site have a verifiable physical "address"?
- Am I seeing the appropriate social signals for a product or service which actually or likely "exists"?

These types of things are all possible to be checked and measured.

Some may not agree with these ranking factors, but you need to think a bit differently or "out-of-the-box" than everyone else, a little less "by-the-book", and a little more artificially intelligent. Consider:

1. *If search engines could measure this sort of thing, would they use it?*
2. *If so, how would they do it?*
3. *If you were designing an algorithm to detect brands, what are the types of things you would look for?*

Identifying these types of things and adding them to your marketing mix would and could only help a site and not hurt it.

For example, adding a link to a site from a reputable source which actually checks a business before giving a link is important. Verifying a business's physical address in a Google trusted source like Google Places can only help, not hurt, so get it out of the way by doing it. This way, if it is a ranking factor, it's done, if not, no loss.

The above is just one sort of way to look at Panda but there is much more to it. Even if search engines are not doing this stuff yet, they are trying their best to do it, and the sooner you start preparing for it, the better off your site, your business, and your overall success will be.

As for the domain aspect of Panda, it is interesting to see that the domain name industry has not reacted in a more heated negative way as Panda specifically undermines the value of keyword driven and generic domain names. Many site owners who have survived on the quality of their domain name alone are learning a hard lesson; that not only will these changes affect their traffic, but they will also affect the value of their domain assets.

So if you want to stay ahead of the pack, it is time to start looking closer at a sites "brand value", not just its links, domain, architectural structure, optimization, etc.

Chapter 20 ("White Hat" and "Black Hat" SEO)

If you've asked about the difference between *"White Hat"* and *"Black Hat"* SEO (Search Engine Optimization), this Chapter's for you.

Simply put, it's about <u>RISK</u>. When it comes to Search Engine Optimization techniques, there are both "white hat" and "black hat" tactics.

A common question among those interested in Search Engine Optimization is simply: *"What's the difference?"* Search Engine Optimization has been revolving around these two *"types"* of techniques, but the question remains for many as to which is the *"right way"* to perform Search Engine Optimization or which way will work best for a business's overall Internet marketing strategy.

First and foremost, you'll want to ensure that you do things which are within Google's webmaster guidelines. Yahoo and Bing have their own rules and these search engines do matter as well, but for the most part, and in my opinion, Google's webmaster guidelines are the *"holy grail"* if you will, of all webmaster rules to follow. This is because Google will equate to the highest percentage of traffic you'll see from any search engine in almost any scenario.

These guidelines provided by Google can be fairly vague and/or complicated at times, but for the most part, they're common sense. Having a great site, a good idea, or a unique service just isn't enough to make it with your Internet business. You need visibility on Google to matter, <u>period</u>. Sites that do well on Google and partner sites will make money and receive lots of traffic, sites which don't, well, they will not.

That's the bottom line.

This image (below) is a visualization of how and why Google.com typically makes and breaks all online businesses. Although this changes a bit from time to time, for the most part, this is generally what you'll see when looking at stats for your average web site.

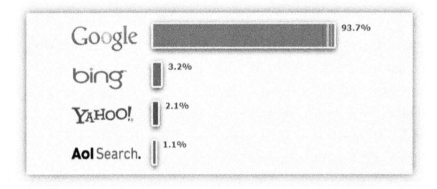

The above web site statistics screenshot is a simple visualization of how and why Google.com typically makes and breaks all online businesses. While we're here, this is also a good visualization and example on why this book primarily focuses on Google.

Whether you're paying Google to appear through pay-per-click advertising with Adwords, or you're highly ranked for search terms important to you, one thing is for sure, unless you're uniquely special in your own way, you'll need a consistent stream of new visitors to 'find' your web site, and without Google, it's just not going to be easy.

Generally speaking, the more aggressive you are when doing Search Engine Optimization, the more risk you'll take on towards the potential of getting your site penalized. Conservative SEO's usually stick with what they know best and what feels right - "*White Hat SEO*".

White hat SEO's or "*White Hats*" tend to produce results that last for long periods of time. This is because they are less risky when it comes to search engine optimization and link building so they are less likely to be impacted by frequent algorithmic updates. Over time, many learn that although "white hat" methods take longer, it is better to take a long-term approach to SEO.

The ultimate goal of Search Engine Optimization shouldn't be just to rank high, but to "maintain high rankings" and traffic growth over time. In order to do that, you're required to assess the risk of everything you do. If you don't understand some of the risks of specific strategies you adopt and use a singularly focused Search Engine Optimization strategy, you'll see wild fluctuating rankings and the risk of losing a significant portion of traffic. Although taking big risks have the potential to reap huge rewards, those rewards are often temporary.

The more balanced your Search Engine Optimization strategy the more stable your rankings will become. "Black Hats" are willing to take that risk and anticipate their sites will get penalized eventually, but often don't care because they can simply register new domain names and start all over again.

If you care about the longevity of your online business, your domain name and/or your client(s), you should care about practicing "*White Hat*" search engine optimization that is within Google's Webmaster Guidelines.

For the most part it's common sense and if your focus is quality and providing value you generally have nothing to worry about.

What makes someone a black hat more specifically?

If they're trying to deceive people by cloaking web pages, hijacking web sites, using hidden text, littering the web with low quality pages or harming a competitor to outrank them in the search results, many call that "*black hat*" Search Engine Optimization because it's employed without regard to others.

Again, "Black Hats" have no regard for user experience or the value and quality of the Internet; the only concern is about making money and receiving traffic.

These are the general differences between "*white hat*" and "*black hat*" Search Engine Optimization, and why White Hat tactics fit better into the ultimate strategy for search engine optimization and marketing your web site online.

What does it mean if someone's a "Gray Hat"?

A "*Gray Hat*", in the search engine optimization community, refers to a skilled optimizer whose activities fall somewhere between white and black on a variety of tactics used. It relates to whether they sometimes arguably act in a way which "bends the envelop" so to speak, though in good will, or to show how to find and disclose vulnerabilities in search engine algorithms, or sometimes employ questionable techniques to optimize sites and otherwise achieve their goals.

Chapter 21 (Pay Per Click (PPC) Advertising)

Pay-Per-Click advertising is a form of advertising where payment is made only when users click on ads which bring them to a web site or page an advertiser designates. Pay Per Click ads are often referred to as PPC (pay-per-click) or CPC (cost per click) ads, and rightfully so, as they cost money each time a user clicks on them. The amount an advertiser pays is determined based on an auction- like system, whereas those who are willing to pay the most per click will gain the most clicks and traffic.

Benefits of Pay Per Click Advertising

Simply put, pay-per-click advertising works immediately. Pay-per-click ads appear the moment you begin the campaign and stop the moment you discontinue funding your account. Pay per click is the only way to ensure or otherwise guarantee that a site will appear on a search engine for a particular term. A well implemented pay-per-click advertising campaign can be very effective and provide an excellent ROI (return on investment) when managed correctly.

Pay per click ads are the ads you see on web sites and search engines that are identified on the ad itself or above and to the right of search results labeled *"sponsored results"*. Pay per click advertising systems also provide excellent user targeting and tracking tools to ensure ads are working at optimal performance. They also provide powerful conversion tracking tools which can greatly help you measure the ratio of which paid ads or keywords are most successful, allowing you to improve the program over time.

How Pay-Per-Click Services Work

When you run ads on a pay-per-click model, it is very important that your ads are keyword written perfectly. A better written ad can often times out-perform an ad written by an inexperienced marketer or novice PPC user.

Why pay-per-click works

This Heat Map displays the F-shaped principle of how web pages are read. This is a graphical representation of where your prospective customers are most likely to click when using Google and other search engines. This data helps you understand the importance of appearing in the higher results as well as the pay-per-click areas. Appearing in these areas greatly increases you're chances of being clicked on.

Here's how it works. Each pay-per-click ad runs on a set of characteristics.

- Maximum Cost Per Click (maximum amount your willing to pay per click)
- Desired Keywords (when to show your ad for related searches)
- Keyword Relevance (how relevant your ads are to the pages they point to)

Some advertisers running their own campaigns forget or simply just do not realize, that keyword relevance plays a role in pay-per-click ads similar to how search engine optimization works with algorithms. The possibility for a competitors ad to run more frequently or even higher in the sponsored results sections then yours is likely even if you are willing to pay a higher Click Through Rate (CTR) for each ad.

How does this happen? This happens by designing a better strategy when creating the actual ads, their landing pages, and how they are written. Each time a page is loaded where ads are set to appear, search engines will automatically decipher what a page is about in order to display relative ads. The ads with the best relevance along with the higher CTR (click through rate) will run first, the others will follow.

An ad for an advertiser willing to pay 1.50 per click may appear more often than your ad, even though you are willing to pay $3.00 and are targeting the same keywords. This happens simply because the competitors ad contains a better set of keywords and/or their landing page is setup for a specific keyword verses a home page targeting many different keywords.

Each ad campaign should be diversified in such a way that each individual ad targets an individual page, based on an individual keyword. Correctly writing your ads can save you money by creating a more likely conversion of seeker to buyer while ensuring your ads are seen by the most possible consumers at the best rates possible.

Many PPC users make the mistake of sending all clicks to their homepage rather than the exact area on their site that user should go. Determining the right pages for the right ads is essential for a successful campaign. Search engines want advertisers to be successful so they continue to run ads. Search engines prefer to run ads with good conversion rates, which works best for them, their users and the advertiser, despite the amount per click your willing to pay.

Chapter 22 (What Is Reputation Management?)

Reputation Management involves both search engine optimization and strategic public relations methods in order to control what users find online when searching for brands in search engines. One negative review or article on your business can change the perception of your entire enterprise for years to come.

In today's vastly social web, businesses can and do suffer from scrupulous competitors, past employees and/or irate customers regardless of the *right or wrong* in the situation.

Unfortunately, there are entire sites dedicated to the production and promotion of negative articles which can act as judge, jury and executioner for your business. Because of this, companies never know when a negative article could show up and impact their company. Business owners should be proactive about their online reputation to ensure positive information on their service is at all times easy to find.

Before a consumer decides to do business they often turn to Google or other search engines to look for testimonials, complaints, reviews and opinions of others who may already have used the company they are considering doing business with. Google makes these reviews easy to find and sometimes even automatically populates a search box with related searches just by beginning to enter a brand, especially for brands that are often searched for with the words "reviews", "scam" and/or "complaints" as shown in the image below.

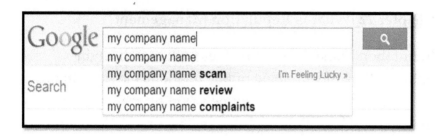

As you type, Google's algorithm predicts and displays search queries based on other users' search activities. For certain queries, Google will show separate predictions for just the last few words. Below the word that you're typing in the search box, you'll see a smaller drop-down list containing predictions based only on the last words of your query. While each prediction shown in the drop-down list has been typed before by Google users, the combination of your primary text along with the completion may be unique.

Predicted queries are algorithmically determined based on a number of purely algorithmic factors (including popularity of search terms) without human intervention. The autocomplete data is updated frequently to offer fresh and rising search queries.

Most businesses do not consider reputation management until it is too late or until they find that an "anonymous" user has posted an article online which is false and affecting their business. They panic and begin the reputation management process which first involves research, shopping and possibly a little trial and error. This costs more than your hard earned money; this costs time, while negative information remains, affecting sales volume and your bottom line.

Be Your Own Reputation Management Consultant

Many companies already possess the positive information needed to complete reputation management services. Awards, new additions to services, involvement with the community, charity work, company updates and new hires can all be used to create, *'spin'* or publicize positive information about your business.

Use these items to publish press releases and news about your business which will both promote your services and protect your brand over time. Well written press releases can do wonders for your business reputation management efforts. They often appear in search engines near the top and can also appear in Google News searches immediately and remain there for weeks at a time. They are also often copied by other sites that look to publish news and information as it hits news and public relations sites.

Don't wait to grab hold of your online reputation until it's too late. Use reputation management methods with your search engine optimization strategy by periodically publishing press releases and news about your business. Including links to your site in press releases can also help support your link building efforts as well.

Writing Your Own Press Releases

A press release, news release, media release or statement is a written communication directed at members of the news media for the purpose of announcing something newsworthy. An effective press release includes a headline, subtitle, body, boilerplate, and contact details.

Basic Press Release Format (Example)

MAIN TITLE OF PRESS RELEASE GOES HERE IN ALL UPPER CASE
Subtitle Goes Here in Title Case (Upper and Lower)

body of press release body of press release body of press release body of press release body of press release body of press release body of press release body of press release body of press release.

body of press release body of press release body of press release body of press release body of press release body of press release body of press release body of press release body of press release body of press release body of press release body of press release body of release body of press release.

body of press release body of press release.

body of press release body of press release body of press release body of press release body of press release.

boilerplate boilerplate boilerplate boilerplate boilerplate boilerplate boilerplate boilerplate boilerplate boilerplate boilerplate boilerplate boilerplate boilerplate boilerplate boilerplate boilerplate.

\# \# \#

If you'd like more information about this topic, or to schedule an interview with John Smith, please call Pat Brown at 555/555-2222 or e-mail Pat at pr@theplace4vitamins.com

Contact: John Smith
Tel. 555/555-2222
Cell Phone: 555/555-2222
Email: johnsmith@anywhere.com

A "boilerplate" is an optional block of text used over and over again each time you publish your press releases which can include a web site URL. You can also use anchor text within the body of your release which will help build valuable backlinks to your site, plus, you'll gain additional backlinks from any sites which copy it.

Chapter 23 (Content Marketing – The New SEO)

Content marketing has been around for some time but has just recently been gaining attention within main stream marketing circles in reference to search engine optimization (SEO). It is often underestimated by even long time professionals in SEO but is a very powerful means of building both inbound links and traffic to your site. The key is creating content based on *"true value"* and user interest so it spreads virally like wild fire through sharing in social media circles.

What It Used To Be

Several years ago many marketers, specifically search engine optimizers, would generate loads of keyword stuffed content about various topics related to products or services they were offering, knowing that search engines would index this content. Based on primitive algorithms, search engines would display these content pages high within search results provided that key terms were found within pages and basic on-page elements were present. This would generate lots of traffic to optimizers web sites based on the amount of content they were publishing and hosting on their sites. The algorithms targeting poor quality content have changed greatly (Panda) which has caused these processes to be much less effective and has effectively cleaned up search engines considerably.

What It Is Today

Today, you see a much more sophisticated approach to content marketing which is more genuine and more effective for marketers when done successfully. True content marketing involves generating high quality content which piques the interest of readers so they're moved by its creatively and authorship, and share it with friends, others and link to it from blog's which cause it to out-perform other pages in search engines that may be similar in focus. This process builds not only back links, but targeted traffic, the most valuable commodity the web can provide.

Contextual Links

One of the best ways to build links for SEO purposes is to obtain *"contextual links"* that are editorial in nature. Contextual links refer to links within the content of a page. These types of links are the most effective for SEO because they're natural to search engines. By getting a contextual link within the body of content in relation to its target web site can reap significant rewards when done right. Target sites can rank for contextual linked anchor text quickly and consistently because search engines trust it more and this makes a huge difference in the score of web pages as well as how much PageRank™ those links may receive. Merit based links within content work much better than most other types of links a site can produce through most advertising or marketing techniques.

The Social Element

There is also a significant value associated with being linked to from social circles. Search engines like Google, Microsoft and Yahoo, have openly admitted that they do use social signals in the algorithms which make up the ranking determinations of their search engines.

Having links to your site on Facebook, Twitter, Google+ as well as other popular social sites is significant as it signals there is *"buzz"* and discussion related to a particular site. Web sites which generate no social activity at all will not see a value of '*social circle actively*' because they are not found within social circles and aren't being mentioned. Having a site referenced in social circles can be compared to the difference of having a web site or not having one - it's clearly better having one than not having one. For search engine optimization, it's better to be mentioned within social circles, than not be mentioned at all.

The Freshness Value

Google specifically has admitted several times over the last year or so that they are adding a value associated with the freshness of content produced as well as more scrutiny on those who are producing it. Newer content is considered, in most cases, more valuable than older content and is moving into search engines faster, even by the minute. Fresh content often out-ranks older content as blog's, news, and the freshness of information is pushed to the forefront of what is found within search. There is a tremendous value put on new information in an effort to make new content easy to find. Those producing fresh quality content will receive a great deal of traffic from the first pages of search engines, specifically Google. Savvy marketing professionals know not to underestimate content marketing in any online advertising strategy.

There are some instances where older content can be ranked higher *(Chapter 30)*, but for the most part, fresh is better.

Chapter 24 (Understanding Semantic Search)

Semantic search seeks to improve search accuracy by understanding searcher intent and the contextual meaning of terms as they appear on the Internet. Below we will evaluate some real examples of Semantic Search in action. It is nothing short of amazing to see how one word can mean another to Google.

Understanding semantic search and how it works can greatly help you to increase the overall visibility of your web site. When Google reads your site, having your most important keywords may not be enough. You may need to go just a bit further and make sure that your keywords AND your keywords "related keywords" are there as well.

Google is also putting great effort into using Semantic Search for determine the meaning of words based on other words in the same body of text or together with a query. For instance, "Orange" may be a fruit, unless the word "Yellow" is also present, in which case, it likely refers to the color "Orange". Or the word "Apple" may be considered a search for fruit unless the word "Computers" is nearby.

Let's look at a few examples of how some words have other meanings to Google using Semantic Indexing.

If you have been using Google for a while, you may have already noticed that Google will **bold** keyword you're searching for when it returns results on the Google search pages. We'll use this bold feature to identify what words Google is using when returning results.

Example #1: In the first example, you'll see an ordinary search performed for the word "Cars" on Google.com. Google returns a search page with the term being searched in **Bold**. Google bolds only the word "**cars**" and it's non plural version "**car**".

Example #2: In Example two, we run a query using the Semantic Search commands which are a ~ (to the left of the "1" key) sign followed by the keyword in question and a - dash) sign followed again by the keyword. This result will show you how Google believes that the word "**marketing**" has something to do with the words "**Business**" "**Market**" and "Media".

To try this, use a ~ (to the left of the "1" key) sign followed by the keyword in question and a – (dash) sign followed again by the keyword as displayed in the image.

The idea, keeping Semantic search in mind, would be that if your main targeted keyword is "Marketing" then having these additional words on your website as well as closely related words may be beneficial to your overall keyword density and semantic relevance.

Semantic search seeks to improve search accuracy by understanding searcher intent and the contextual meaning of terms as they appear when users type in the search box, to generate more relevant results.

Semantic Search systems consider various points including context of search, location, intent, variation of words, synonyms, generalized and specialized queries, concept matching and natural language queries to provide relevant search results. Major web search engines like Google, Yahoo and Bing try to incorporate some elements of Semantic Search as best they can and this will likely both improve and increase over time.

Let's look at another few examples.

Example #3: In Example three, we again run a query using the Semantic Search commands which are a ~ (to the left of the "1" key) sign followed by the keyword in question and a - dash) sign followed again by the keyword. This result will show you how Google believes that the word "**cheap**" has something to do with or is closely related to the words "**Discount**" or to "**Buy**" something.

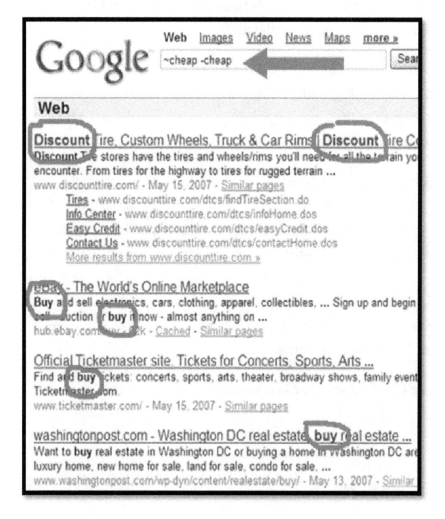

Latent Semantic Indexing (LSI) is an indexing and retrieval method that uses a mathematical technique called Singular value decomposition (SVD) to identify patterns in the relationships between the terms and concepts contained in an unstructured collection of text.

Latent Semantic Indexing is based on the principle that words that are used in the same contexts tend to have similar meanings. A key feature of LSI is its ability to extract the conceptual content of a body of text by establishing associations between those terms that occur in similar contexts.

It's called Latent Semantic Indexing because of its ability to correlate semantically related terms that are latent (present but not visible, apparent, or actualized) in a collection of text. The method is also called latent semantic analysis (LSA), uncovers the underlying latent semantic structure in the usage of words in a body of text and how it can be used to extract the meaning of the text in response to user queries, commonly referred to as concept searches.

We'll wrap up this chapter with another good example of Semantic Search in action.

Example #4: In Example four, we again run a query using the Semantic Search commands which are a ~ (to the left of the "1" key) sign followed by the keyword in question and a - (dash) sign followed again by the keyword. This result will show you how Google believes that the phrase "**Real Estate**" has something to do with or is closely related to the words "**Property**", "**Estate**", "**Home**" and "**Homes for Sale**".

Pretty interesting isn't it?

Google likely uses these and/or similar techniques when it reads and comprehends your web pages. It is also likely used when deciphering anchor text within links that point to your site or throughout your sites' inter-linking page structure.

So when using keywords on your web site, as well as while link building, it may be very beneficial for you to not only cover your most important targeted keywords, but to include some of those closely related terms that could give your overall "Latent Semantic" Keyword Density a higher score.

Latent Semantic Indexing (LSI) is being used in a variety of information retrieval and text processing applications, although its primary application has been for concept searching and automated document categorization. It is an amazing science that is helping make search more reliable, accurate and easy to use. This too will likely improve and increase over time.

Chapter 25 (Website Monetization)

There is one fact about generating revenue with your web site: Those who make the most money usually have the largest audience (the most traffic).

Although there are several ways to monetize a web site, there is only one fundamental requirement to making your site generate revenue, and that's **TRAFFIC**.

No web site, regardless of how great it may seem on the surface, or how excellently designed it is, can possibly be expected to make anyone any money at all if it doesn't have any traffic coming in. It doesn't matter as much where the traffic is coming from (search engines, links, etc.), but it must, in fact, exist.

Whether your site is visited through search engines, directly typed in the address bar, or visited through links from other sites, it does not make too much of a difference as long as people are getting there. Have you got a web site with traffic? If so, what you actually have is a business, and it is up to you to know the best way to convert that traffic into revenue.

How you choose to monetize your site can make all the difference in the amount of time and energy you'll need to put in and how much money those efforts will ultimately turn into. A great site, monetized correctly, does most the work for you. On the other side of the coin, a site not monetized correctly will have you chasing your tail, putting in lots of hours of hard work, with very little reward.

Many beginners give up before they reach success because they used the wrong methods - not because their idea wasn't realistic. Any idea can be a great one, but the process of monetization must not be flawed.

Lead Generation

A popular way developers can monetize a web site is through lead generation. Leads can either be direct phone calls to a business or they can be email contacts to be followed up on.

Most lead generation sites will have contact forms or other user input areas to capture a visitors contact information so that their initial interest can be utilized by a "closer" (an experienced sales person) who then turns them into a paying customer.

Many web sites sell leads to eager parties willing to buy them, while others may benefit only from a percentage of sales generated based on the lead.

Other sites may use affiliate programs to turn leads into commissions dynamically through a referral link to another site where the referral link is recorded and on a conversion, electronically delivers successful transaction record for the affiliate marketer. A commission is then attributed to his or her affiliate account so that they can get paid for that referral.

Leads can be valuable to both buyer and seller depending on the industry and agreements. A web site which generates good targeted leads can be worth a lot of money to businesses who purchase similar leads.

Direct Sales

Having items for sale on your web site is one of the most direct and easiest to understand ways of making money from your web site. Products can be as simple as a digital or downloadable file (like this book in its digital form for instance) or as complicated as a product to be built, shipped, and delivered through conventional means like the postal service or courier.

Direct sales can also refer to the filling of advertising space on a web site by communicating with interested businesses who are seeking visibility on a particular web site. If a web site has lots of targeted traffic, getting business owners or others who need traffic interested in advertising is easy, and many times the inquiries to appear on the site come directly to you from traffic hungry advertisers.

Advertising Networks

Advertising Networks or Ad networks are companies who have large numbers of clients looking to run their banners or text ads across networks of web properties. These companies usually service both "advertisers" and "publishers".

Advertisers are those who want their ads to run, and publishers are web site operators who allow space to be filled on their sites with advertising. The ad networks serve as a middle man or go-between for both advertiser and publisher.

Ad networks are great for publishers because they eliminate the need to search for advertisers; for publishers they eliminate the need to search for space available for ads.

Ad networks collect fees from advertisers and pay a portion of those fees to the publisher who actually serves the ads. Publishers are paid based on either how many times an ad is displayed (CPM – cost per impressions) or clicked on (CPC – cost per click), and sometimes even how effective the ads convert (CPA – cost per action). Ad networks are generally the preferred choice for web site operators who lack their own sales teams or representatives.

Below is a list of advertising networks based in the U. S.

- AdBrite.com
- AdKnowledge.com
- AdSense.Google.com
- Bidvertiser.com
- Blogads.com
- Chitika.com
- Clickbooth.com
- DoubleClick.com
- EpicAdvertising.com
- Infolinks.com
- Kontera.com
- RealTechNetwork.com
- RightMedia.com
- TribalFusion.com
- ValueClick.com
- VoloMedia.com
- Zedo.com

Affiliate Programs

Affiliate marketing is a marketing practice in which a business rewards an affiliate for each customer brought about by the affiliate's marketing efforts. Affiliate marketing overlaps with other Internet marketing methods to some degree, because affiliates often use regular advertising methods. Those methods include organic search engine optimization, paid search engine marketing, e-mail marketing, and in some sense display advertising. On the other hand, affiliates sometimes use less orthodox techniques, such as publishing reviews (sometimes fake) of products or services offered by a partner.

Below is a list of affiliate networks based in the U.S.:

- Amazon.com
- eBayPartnerNetwork.com
- MarketHealth.com
- Clickbank.com
- CommissionJunction.com
- SellHealth.com
- ShareASale.com
- LinkShare.com

Eighty percent of affiliate programs today use revenue sharing or cost per sale (CPS - you get paid when a sale is made) as a compensation method, nineteen percent use cost per action (CPA – you get paid when a form is filled out or a specific user action is made), and the remaining programs use other methods such as cost per click (CPC – you get paid when a user clicks an ad).

My personal favorite is "Google AdSense". I prefer AdSense because it's simple to add to your site, it doesn't slow down your page load time, the ads are perfectly targeted to page content, the shape and style of ads are fully controllable, it's easy to track, and for me, it's paid the best.

Google AdSense is a program run by Google Inc. that allows publishers in the Google Network of content sites (your site, when you sign up and get accepted) to serve "automatic" text, image, video, and rich media advertisements that are targeted to site content and audience.

The keyword here is "automatic" which means you do not need to pick and choose advertisers, of course, unless you want to. These advertisements are administered, sorted, and maintained by Google, and they generate revenue on either a per-click or per-impression basis.

Another reason I prefer Google AdSense specifically is due to the ease of adding sites to your portfolio as you're not required to get new sites approved before you can install your ad code. Google allows ads to run automatically as soon as your publisher ad code is installed. The AdSense system automatically determines the most relevant, targeted and profitable ads to display.

It's very easy to get started with Google AdSense and it only takes a few minutes. You'll fill out one single online application and that's it. Once you're approved, all you have to do is copy and paste a designated block of HTML into your site and targeted ads will start showing up on your website automatically. It couldn't be more simple.

Application Process

Google AdSense

Help

Search AdSense Help

Welcome to AdSense What is AdSense? | Already have an account?
Please complete the application form below

Website Information

Website URL: [?]
• Please list your primary URL only.
• Example: www.example.com

Website language Select a language:
• Tell us your website's primary language to help our review process.

☐ I will not place ads on sites that include incentives to click on ads.

☐ I will not place ads on sites that include pornographic content.

Contact Information

Account type: [?] Select an account type

Country or territory: United States

⚠ **Important** - Your payment will be sent to the address below. Please complete all fields that apply to your address, such as a full name, full street name and house or apartment number, and accurate country, ZIP code, and city. Example.

Payee name (full name):
• Your Payee name needs to match the name on your bank account.
• Payee must be at least 18 years of age to participate in AdSense.

Street Address:

City/Town:

State: Select state

ZIP: [?]

UNITED STATES
• To change your country or territory please change your selection at the top of this form.

☐ I agree that I can receive checks made out to the payee name I have listed above.

Telephone Numbers
Phone:

Email preference We'll send you service announcements that relate to your agreement with Google.
☑ In addition, send me periodic newsletters with tips and best practices and occasional surveys to help Google improve AdSense.

Policies

AdSense applicants must agree to adhere to AdSense program policies (details)
☐ I agree that I will not click on the Google ads I'm serving through AdSense.
☐ I certify that I have read the AdSense Program Policies.
☐ I do not already have an approved AdSense account. (Click here if you do.)

Submit Information

Site operators can apply for an account at:
http://www.google.com/adsense

Chapter 26 (Measuring Traffic and Statistics)

Google Analytics is a free statistics program offered by Google to users who have Google accounts. Google Analytics is free but with everything free there is always something in it for the provider. For Google, having a deep understanding of your traffic and users habits while on your site is extremely important to them, so Google offers this "free tool" in exchange for that data.

Google Analytics is an exceptional tool for Webmasters willing to share their web sites information with Google in order to use the Analytics system. Google Analytics records and reports valuable traffic statistics including:

- Content Analytics - Helps you understand which parts of your website are performing well or which pages are most popular.
- Social Analytics - Measures how visitors interact with sharing features on your site and engage with your content across social platforms.
- Mobile Analytics - Measures the impact of mobile on your business. If you offer mobile apps Analytics measures how people use your app.
- Conversion Analytics - Find out how many customers you're attracting, how much you're selling and how users covert on your site.
- Advertising Analytics - Links your website activity to your marketing campaigns to help you improve your advertising performance.
- Analysis Tools - Decide what data you want to view and customize your reports, with just a few clicks.

Google Analytics can also be set to provide reports on your traffic or any particular charicteristic your monitoring. These reports can be set via email to any address you designate and automatically delivered either daily, weekly, monthly or on any desired interval. Simply set these preferences from your Google Analytics account.

Google Analytics Dashboard

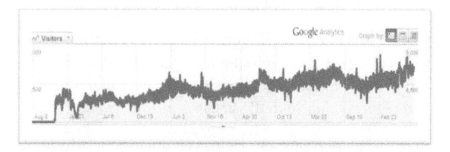

Google account holders can sign up for a free account here: http://www.google.com/analytics/

Public Traffic Data: Alexa.com

Alexa provides information about websites including Top Sites, Internet Traffic Stats and Metrics, Related Links, Online Reviews and Contact Information (Archived WhoIs Data)

For publically available "hint" of a specific sites' traffic you can try using www.Alexa.com. It only acquires data from users who actually have the Alexa toolbar installed on their browser, and thus it is impossible for it to be completely accurate – but it is a free tool available online and will provide interesting information and a quick glimpse at top Internet sites or how busy someone else's web site might be.

Chapter 27 (Local Search and Google Maps)

Local listings on Google and other search engines are essential to your business. Research suggests that over 80% of Internet users search for local listings using search engines like Google. Simply put, this means that if your business is not listed within local search in addition to the regular index of sites, you're likely missing out on most of the sales you can generate from new customers.

Local sections of search engines are driving the majority of sales and traffic to local businesses through advanced technology like "*localization*" which identifies where a user actually is, geographically, when conducting a search. This helps search engines deliver local listings without the user having to type where they are, or where they're searching for it. Ever wonder why some listings appear with a map, but not you? Those businesses are using "*localization*" to their advantage, in ways that connect them with local customers using the Internet. Again, that's 80% of the people who might do business with you.

While having your business listed in print Yellow Pages or other offline traditional media does work, it's not what it once was - by a land slide. For example, specific research on the Yellow Pages industry itself shows a steady

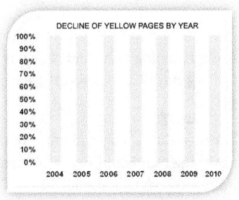

decline in the actual usage of print Yellow Pages within a year to year timeline since 2004.

This is catastrophic for the Yellow Pages industry, but great news for businesses like you who are ready to identify ways to save money while generating more leads. This is done by taking what you already spend from one vertical and effectively spending those same marketing dollars in another.

A full page ad in the printed Yellow Pages could reasonably cost your business between 3k - 5k thousand dollars per month while fetching just a fraction of the response it once did due to these changes in user habits.

Ask yourself this: Would you expect it to be as effective as say a #1 listing on Google Local in your region, viewable 24 hours a day, 7 days a week, from a computer or even a cell phone?

Don't continue to spend your marketing dollars in print, while the number of people who are available to see those ads continues to decline.

It is just "smart marketing" to thoroughly evaluate your actual ROI (Return On Investment) and conversion rates on different channels of advertising efforts, especially when things tighten up. This will help you turn the same marketing dollars into more leads, more traffic, and ultimately more business.

What are search engines looking for?

- Accurate, verifiable and up-to-date listing information.
- Relevance to what a user is searching for.
- Ratings, reviews and other social signals.
- Verification that your business, in fact, exists at a particular location.

If your web site isn't appearing in local searches (maps listings) or not appearing where you wish it would you need to focus on submitting it to local search engines like Google Maps (it's free).

1) submit your business to local portions of search engines.
2) verifying your information and business address

Be sure to completely fill out your business profile page and try to get customers to place a review if you have one on there. From what I have seen, Google has a tendency to display Maps listings based on how complete they are. If your listing has little content, few images, comments, videos business hours, etc., to display, Google will tend to show other listings which are more complete to offer the visitor more information.

To submit your local business to Google visit:
www.google.com/places/

Chapter 28 (What's Happening Now?)

The last year or so has paved the way for many changes in the field of search engine marketing. In particular, since around August 10th 2010, Yahoo and Bing began to share the same "SERPS" which are provided by Microsoft. Google has also been getting much more aggressive about their updates and algorithm changes. It could be totally unrelated, but it does sort of feel like a real change took place over there when Co-Founder Larry Page took over as CEO on April 4th, 2011.

Looking back, domain names took some heat in December 2010 as Google publically released that they would reduce the benefit to sites based on keywords in the domain alone. Then, in February, Google released "Panda" a direct target for content generation and webmasters taking advantage of pumping out content too quickly. This seemed to be where brand power really came into play. Social media awareness grew significantly all through 2011 and is moving quickly to the forefront of optimization even today. We also saw Google encrypt search referrals and publicly releasing that they make in the area of 200 changes per year to the algorithm and claim they intend to be more transparent about the changes they do make, when they do so, and why - but of course, they'll never expose their secret sauce.

In March of 2012, Google officially announced the release of the latest update to its major algorithm dubbed "Panda". The change was specifically targeted at Search Engine Optimization and aimed to *level the playing field* so that webmasters who focus solely on SEO would see diminished rankings to make room for those who don't.

Here is a timeline of all tweaks since Panda was released:

- Panda 3.5 on April 19th
- Panda 3.4 on March 23rd
- Panda 3.3 on February 26th
- Panda 3.2 on January 15th
- Panda 3.1 on November 18th
- Panda 2.5.3 on October 19th
- Panda 2.5.2 on October 13th
- Panda 2.5.1 on October 9th
- Panda 2.5 on September 28th
- Panda 2.4 on August 14th
- Panda 2.3 on July 21nd
- Panda 2.2 on June 17th
- Panda 2.1 on May 9th
- Panda 2.0 on April 12th
- Panda 1.0 on February 24th

This latest update included a new "over optimization" penalty where Google targets sites with too many low quality links (unnatural or paid for). Sites which target specific anchor text too heavily wind up not ranking well at all for those phrases, so diversifying your anchor text is extremely important or more important than ever if you're doing any link building. You cannot purchase links to your site on autopilot. You must ensure your methods are as natural as possible.

Hundreds of thousands of low quality sites and blogs were and are still being removed from the Google index due to the sale and exchange of links which creates low quality sites and pages all over the web. These pages exist only to host links for search optimizers and web marketers link buying and trading efforts and Google isn't having it anymore.

If you're hammering your anchor texts or supporting the creation and existence of low quality pages with your efforts or ad dollars, you might want to hold onto your hat. It's not like Google wants to have to clean up the entire Internet, but unfortunately, their just stuck with project. I mean, people have come to expect them to be so good at what they do, how are they supposed to deal with these people that just "litter" their Internet with junk?

Have you ever seen a web site which is purchased and hosted by some link marketing company only for the purpose of selling links ads on it. It seems they littler the page with links to the maximum amount of littering possible and then move on to their next host. This just creates hundreds of thousands of garbage web sites and web pages all over the Internet and it's coming to an end. But web marketers will continue until it no longer works, which is why if Google and other search engines want to put a stop to it, it's best to first stop rewarding it. But it appears Google will go a bit further and take action by removing host sites and penalizing ad purchasers.

I think in a way, the spam team at Google must feel like someone has come over their house at night and just dumped their garbage pails on the front lawn and ran away, Google is going to hide on the side of the house at night and come out and 'stick em' so they do not come back anymore. If this happens to you, go back to *Chapter 6* ☺.

Chapter 29 (The Google Patent Interpretation)

It is interesting to watch when Google begins to roll out new algorithmic technologies, not only for how it effects the Internet and "Search" overall, but how it effects themselves as a company and a business.

When Google updates their algorithms with significant changes, they also update their patents and/or file for new patents to include claims which support new methods they develop and decide to include. According to the U.S. Patent and Trademark Office, Google has been assigned over 720 patents, mostly for search engine technology.

As Google files these patents Google becomes the exclusive owner of these identified methods which, in most cases, eliminates other competing search engines like Bing and Yahoo from using the exact described and claimed methods thus making it extremely difficult for these competitors to utilize the exact strategies, even if eventually discovered. Competitors are then left to develop their own or different ways to justify the same means which may not easily be more, equal to or even nearly effective.

Included in the following of this book are my theories and interpretations of several claims for Google patents which are related to their search engine algorithm.

By reading each claim carefully and closely looking at the technologies that Google seeks to protect, it does reveal a limited glimpse into the thoughts of their best minds at work; Google's senior engineers describe what it is they are seeking to accomplish with their algorithm and how they explain the process intended to be used and protected.

Most of these patent claims and technologies are likely to already be in use, and some still in development, but again, this gives what would be the clearest look into what's coming next from the world's best search engine and leading Internet traffic provider.

I would like to again point out that these are "opinions" and are not necessarily "factual" or "accurate" and, as opinion, may change often due to the nature of the Internet, search engines, current or recent evolving trends, new information I discover or further case studies which become available.

This information including my "opinions" on these patents I explain and go into detail on here could easily be misinterpreted. My "opinions" in this document are not designed to provide you with professional advice. Should you take action or incorporate such opinions on your own behalf or the behalf of a third party, you acknowledge that you do so at your own risk.

Note: From here on in this book, excluding the final pages, Copyright is claimed only on the boxed interpretation areas immediately underneath each claim which contain my opinion and interpretation, including original and clear written commentary on the public information herein. Additionally, I have underlined and bolded the words and sections of each claim I feel best support my interpretation areas. Google Inc. is the owner of these claims and they are filed and on record with the United States Patent and Trademark Office which can be accessed here: http://www.uspto.gov/patents/process/search/

United States Patent
Application
Kind Code
Acharya; Anurag ;   et al.

20110264671

A1

October 27, 2011

DOCUMENT SCORING BASED ON DOCUMENT CONTENT UPDATE

Abstract

A system may determine a measure of **how a content of a document changes over time, generate a score for the document** based, at least in part, on the measure of how the content of the document changes over time, and rank the document with regard to at least one other document based, at least in part, on the score.

"A documents importance, relevance, value, as well as the attributes (its score) related with the document can change and/or change other documents (possibly the documents which are linked to or documents which are linked from) depending on the documents freshness."

Inventors: **Acharya; Anurag**; *(Campbell, CA)* **; Cutts; Matt;** *(Mountain View, CA)* ; **Dean; Jeffrey**; *(Palo Alto, CA)* ; **Haahr; Paul**; *(San Francisco, CA)* ; **Henzinger; Monika**; *(Corseaux, CH)* ; **Hoelzie; Urs**; *(Palo Alto, CA)* ; **Lawrence; Steve**; *(Mountain View, CA)* ; **Pfleger; Karl**; *(Mountain View, CA)* ; **Sercinoglu; Olcan**; *(Mountain View, CA)* ; **Tong; Simon**; *(Mountain View, CA)*

Assignee: **GOOGLE INC.**
Mountain View
CA

Serial No.: **174304**
Series   **13**

Code:

Filed: **June 30, 2011**

Current U.S. Class: **707/749**; 707/E17.009

Class at Publication: **707/749**; 707/E17.009

International Class: G06F 17/30 20060101 G06F017/30

Claims

1-34. (canceled)

> *"Claims 1 – 31 mentioned above have been removed or added within the following claims beginning at 35. This Patent Application has changed at least seven (7) times from when it was originally filed, which has led to claims 1-34 being removed or combined into other claims. This Patent Application also includes references to Patent No. 6,285,999 (Method for Node Ranking in a Linked Database (PageRank) [Inventor: Lawrence Page] filed as early as Jan 9, 1998 Patented on September 4,*

35. A system, comprising: one or more devices to: determine a set of topics associated with a document; **identify, over a time period, <u>how much the set of topics has changed</u>** during the time period; generate a score for the document based on how much the set of topics, associated with the document, has changed during the time period; and rank the document with regard to at least one other document based on the score.

> *"A system or process to decipher how many changes have been made to a document, as well as the significance of that change and to measure whether or not the topic remains similar to the original and/or whether or not any change should affect other documents, likely documents which are linked to or documents which are linked from."*

36. The system of claim 35, where the one or more devices are further to: **identify a spike in a quantity of topics in the set of topics**; and **classify the document as spam** upon identifying the spike in the quantity of topics in the set of topics.

> *"Identify Spikes In Content: A process which identifies sites pushing documents too quickly in comparison to their frequency in a previous timeframe and possibly flag these as spam if new quickly released documents are not signaling some sort of value (possibly by acquiring links)."*

37. The system of claim 36, where when generating the score, the one or more devices are to: **alter the score based on classifying the document as spam**.

> *"If the flagged document is found to be spam, the system will lower the score of the document."*

38. The system of claim 35, where when determining the set of topics associated with the document, the one or more devices are to use at least one of: a categorization of the document, a **Universal Resource Locator (URL) analysis** of the document, an **analysis of content** of the document, a clustering of the document, or a **summarization of the document**.

> *"A function which examines the URL to see if this document and/or any changes to the document from claim 35 would suggest that it is still related to the URL or is related to other documents on this URL based on an overall summary of the document or recent changes to the document."*

39. The system of claim 35, where the one or more devices are further to: **detect a removal of a topic that was previously associated with the document**; and <u>**classify the document as spam**</u> upon detecting the removal of the topic that was previously associated with the document.

> *"A process to closely examine a document which has changed so significantly whereas it suggests the page has been possibly taken over by another party or is being used for an entirely different reason from what the page, which already has a certain authority, was originally created for and whether or not it should lose that authority due to the extent of change which has taken place."*

40. The system of claim 39, where the generated score is a first score, where the one or more devices are further to: <u>**generate a second score**</u>, for the document, that is **based on a relevance of the document to a search query**; and **combine the first and second scores** to generate an <u>**overall score**</u>, where when ranking the document, the one or more devices are to rank the document with regard to at least one other document based on the <u>**overall score**</u>.

> *"A process to allow a document to have two (2) scores, a first score which is based on the document itself and a second score which is based on the search query (which could be measured by use or bounce rate). This process is to then generate an overall score for the document which may affect another document (the document responsible for ranking it or a document linked to)."*

41. The system of claim 40, where when **combining the first and second scores**, the one or more devices are to: <u>**adjust the second score by an amount that is based on the first score**</u>.

> *"When the process of combining the two scores for the overall score, the second score (the usability score) should be adjusted based more on the first score (the document score)."*

42. A method performed by one or more devices, the method comprising: determining, by at least one of the one or more devices, a set of topics associated with a document; **identifying,** by at least one of the one or more devices and **over a time period, how much the set of topics has changed during the time period**; generating, by at least one of the one or more devices, **a score for the document based on <u>how much the set of topics, associated with the document, has changed during the time period</u>**; and ranking, by at least one of the one or more devices, the document with regard to at least one other document based on the score.

> *"A process to allow a score to be determined based on the significance and frequency of changes to the content. Documents which may not change as significantly or as often may be scored less than documents which change frequently and significantly. A documents change (freshness) has the ability to effect at least one other document (possibly documents they link to or vice versa)."*

43. The method of claim 42, further comprising: **identifying a spike in a quantity of topics** in the set of topics; and **<u>classifying the document as spam</u>** upon identifying the spike in the quantity of topics in the set of topics.

> *"A process which identifies "spikes" in the quantity of documents can flag a document for further scrutiny. It appears spikes in the quantity of topic or sets of topics is of significant concern.*

44. The method of claim 43, where generating the score comprises: **altering the score based on <u>classifying the document as spam</u>**.

> *"If process 43 determines the document is spam, this results in an adjustment to lower the score.*

45. The method of claim 42, where determining the set of topics associated with the document is based on at least one of: a categorization of the document, a **Universal Resource Locator (URL)** analysis of the document, an **<u>analysis of content of the document</u>**, a clustering of the document, or a summarization of the document.

> *"A process to determine whether a change to a document (the content) is still related to the previous topic or the URL. Possibly a target for meaningless blog posts, review posts, pre-sell pages or content added or changed only to add links to it or without true regard to editorial discretion."*

46. The method of claim 42, further comprising: **detecting a removal of a topic that was previously associated with the document;** and **<u>classifying the document as spam</u> upon detecting the removal of the topic** that was previously associated with the document.

> *"A process to determine whether the content removed was so significant to the score of the document that the document is now labeled spam (and score the document accordingly *42).*

47. The method of claim 46, where the generated score is a first score, the method further comprising: **generating a second score, for the document,** that is based on a **relevance of the document to a search query**; and **combining the first and second scores to generate an overall score**, where ranking the document includes ranking the document with regard to at least one other document based on the overall score.

> *"A process to determine whether a document is still relevant despite the change by measuring its performance from search queries whereas the query score is the second score which when added to the first score will affect the overall score. Documents scores have the ability to effect at least one other document (possibly the documents they link to or are linked*

48. The method of claim 47, where combining the first and second scores includes: **adjusting the second score by an amount that is based on the first score**.

> *"The stronger the first score, the less effect the second score should have on the overall score."*

49. A computer-readable memory device storing programming instructions that are executable by one or more processors of one or more devices, the programming instructions comprising: one or more instructions to determine a set of topics associated with a document; one or more instructions to **identify, over a time period, how much the set of topics has changed during the time period;**

one or more instructions to **generate a score for the document based on how much the set of topics**, associated with the document, **has changed during the time period;** and one or more instructions to rank the document with regard to at least one other document based on the score.

> *"A process to measure and store the significance of changes to the document over time and generate a score for the document based on whether or not the document remains relevant ."*

50. The computer-readable memory device of claim 49, where the programming instructions further comprise: one or more instructions to **identify a spike in a quantity of topics in the set of topics;** and one or more instructions to **classify the document as spam** upon identifying the spike in the quantity of topics in the set of topics.

> *"A process which identifies "spikes" (too much too fast) in the quantity of documents can flag a document as spam. Spikes in the quantity of topics or sets of topics is again of significant concern."*

51. The computer-readable memory device of claim 50, where the one or more instructions to generate the score include: one or more instructions to **alter the score based on classifying the document as spam**.

> *"A process to alter (lower) the score of a document if measured changes are determined to be spam."*

52. The **computer-readable memory device** of claim 49, where the one or more instructions to determine the set of topics associated with the document include one or more instructions to determine the set of topics based on: a categorization of the document, a Universal Resource Locator (URL) **analysis of the document, an analysis of**

content of the document, a clustering of the document, or a summarization of the document.

> *"A process to identify and measure over time if the overall topic of a document has changed. If so, this process will determine if the content still remains relevant to the URL despite the changes."*

53. The **computer-readable memory device** of claim 49, where the programming instructions further comprise: one or more instructions to **detect a removal of a topic that was previously associated with the document**; and one or more instructions to **classify the document as spam upon detecting the removal** of the topic that was previously associated with the document.

> *"A process to determine whether the content removed is significantly different (in topic and relevance) to the content which replaced it; if not label the document spam."*

54. The **computer-readable memory device** of claim 53, where the generated score is a first score, where the programming instructions further comprise: one or more instructions to generate a second score, for the document, that is based on a relevance of the document to a search query; and one or more instructions to **combine the first and second scores to generate an overall score**, where the one or more instructions to rank the document include one or more instructions to rank the document with regard to at least one other document based on the overall score.

> *"When the first score (content) is combined with the second score (query relevance) create an overall score which is then used to rank the document and allow this process to further include instructions to alter at least one other document (possibly documents it links to or from)."*

55. The **computer-readable memory device** of claim 54, where the one or more instructions to **combine the first and second scores** include: one or more instructions to **adjust the second score by an amount that is based on the first score**.

> *"A process to allow the second score to be influenced primarily by the first score, so it isn't necessarily an average of the two scores; the overall score is effected less by the second score."*

Description

RELATED APPLICATION

[0001] This application is a divisional of **U.S. patent application, Ser. No. 10/748,664, filed Dec. 31, 2003**, which claims priority under 35 U.S.C. .sctn.119 based on U.S. Provisional Application No. 60/507,617, filed Sep. 30, 2003, the disclosures of which are incorporated herein by reference.

THE FOLLOWING PATENT APPLICATIONS:
"Information retrieval based on historical data",
"Systems and methods for determining document
freshness", "Document scoring based on document
inception date", "Document scoring based on query
analysis", "Reviewing the suitability of websites for
participation in advertising", "Document scoring
based on traffic associated with a document",
"Methods and systems for assisted network
browsing", "Methods and systems for establishing a
keyword utilizing path", "System and method for
providing on-line user-assisted Web-based
advertising", "Methods and systems for selecting a
language for text segmentation", "Methods and
systems for augmenting a token lexicon", "Methods
and systems for improving text segmentation" and
"Document scoring based on link based criteria" are
related to this patent: "DOCUMENT SCORING
BASED ON DOCUMENT CONTENT UPDATE" and
as such are referenced here.

BACKGROUND OF THE INVENTION

[0002] 1. Field of the Invention

"A basic statement of the field of "art" (skill or
mastery) to which the invention pertains."

[0003] The present invention relates generally to
information retrieval systems and, more particularly, to
systems and methods for generating search results based,
at least in part, on historical data associated with relevant
documents.

"The invention is a process to generate search engine
results based on the history of web pages."

[0004] 2. Description of Related Art

> *"These claims will describe the "art" (skill or mastery) of the invention and how it works."*

[0005] The World Wide Web ("web") contains a vast amount of information. **Search engines assist users in locating desired portions of this information by <u>cataloging web documents</u>**. Typically, in response to a user's request, a search engine returns links to documents relevant to the request.

> *"The basic description of how a search engine works."*

[0006] Search engines may base their determination of the user's interest on search terms (called a search query) provided by the user. **The goal of a search engine is to <u>identify links to high quality relevant results based on the search query</u>**. Typically, the search engine accomplishes this by matching the terms in the search query to a corpus of pre-stored web documents. Web documents that contain the user's search terms are considered "hits" and are returned to the user.

> *"A basic description of how a search engine measures document data and displays results."*

[0007] Ideally, a search engine, in response to a given user's search query, will provide the user with the **most relevant results**. One category of **<u>search engines identifies relevant documents</u>** based on a comparison of the search query terms to the words contained in the documents. Another category of search engines **<u>identifies</u> relevant documents**

using factors other than, or in addition to, the presence of the **search query terms in the documents**. One such search engine uses information associated with links to or from the documents to determine the relative importance of the documents.

> *"The basic description of keyword density and how links can also be used to determine relevance."*

[0008] Both categories of search engines strive to provide high quality results for a search query. **There are several factors that may affect the quality of the results generated by a search engine**. For example, **some web site producers use spamming techniques to artificially inflate their rank**. Also, "stale" documents (i.e., those documents that have not been updated for a period of time and, thus, contain stale data) may be ranked higher than "**fresher**" documents (i.e., those documents that have been more recently updated and, thus, contain more recent data). In some particular contexts, the higher ranking **stale documents degrade the search results**.

> *"Discussing the idea that stale or old documents may degrade the quality of search results. Documents that have not been updated in a period of time or are not determined to be fresh, may still rank high but are not good for search engines to continue to allow to rank well. This also highlights the fact that spamming techniques are used intentionally to rank documents higher."*

[0009] Thus, there remains a **need to improve the quality of results** generated by search engines.

> *"This requires search engines to find a way to display only the most relevant and fresh results."*

SUMMARY OF THE INVENTION

[0010] Systems and methods consistent with the principles of **the invention may score documents based, at least in part, on history data** associated with the documents. This scoring may be used to improve search results generated in connection with a search query.

> *"This defines the desire to use historical data in relation to ranking documents in search engines and basically explains the purpose of the invention which is to improve search results."*

TAKE HISTORY INTO CONSIDERATION.

[0011] According to one aspect, a method may include determining a measure of **how a content of a document changes over time**; generating a score for the document based, at least in part, on the measure of how the content of the document changes over time; and ranking the document with regard to at least one other document based, at least in part, on the score.

> *"A process to allow a score to be determined based on measuring and recording how a documents content changes over time while also allowing this ability which measured change to effect at least one other document (possibly the documents they link to or are linked from) based on that score."*

[0012] According to another aspect, a method may include **determining a first rate of change** in a content of a document in a first time period; <u>determining a second rate of change</u> in the content of the document in a second time period; <u>comparing</u> the first rate of change and the second rate of change to determine whether there is an **increase or a decrease** in the rate of change in the content of the document; **generating a score** for the document based, at least in part, **on whether there is an increase or a decrease in the rate of change** in the content of the document; and ranking the document with regard to at least one other document based, at least in part, on the score.

> *"A process to determine the date of changes to a document, the frequency and rate of changes over a period of time and then examine the frequency and rate of change within different timeframes to determine if the rate of change is slowing down or picking-up) while also allowing the ability to effect at least one other document (the documents they link to or are linked from)."*

[0013] According to yet another aspect, a method may include receiving a search query; performing a search based, at least in part, on the search query to **identify a group of search result documents**; determining a date on which a content changed for each of the search result documents in a set of the search result documents in the group; <u>determining an average date-of-change of the search result documents</u> in the set of search result documents based, at least in part, on the determined dates; generating a score for a search result document in the set of search result documents based, at least in part, on a difference between the determined date associated with the search result document and the **average date-of-change** of the search result documents in the set of search result documents; and ranking the search result document with regard to at least one other one of the search result documents based, at least in part, on the score.

"A process to determine the "fresher" results. There is a desire to display the "freshest" documents out of similar documents which are displayed in search results. So if there are groups of search results which are very similar the rate and frequency of change will affect how that rank. Documents which are updated often and/or deemed fresher will likely out rank other documents."

[0014] According to a further aspect, a method may include **determining** a measure of **how anchor text associated with a link pointing to a document changes over time; generating a score for the document** based, at least in part, on the measure of how the anchor text associated with the **link pointing to the document changes over time**; and ranking the document with regard to at least one other document based, at least in part, on the score.

"A process to determine when the anchor text of a link changes over time and attempt to decipher why it has changed. Changes in anchor text should be associated with a change in the document it links to. Changes in anchor text which are not supported by a change in its target could be questionable or be flagged as a manipulative tactic. Determinations may effect at least one other document (possibly the documents they link to or are linked from)."

[0015] According to another aspect, a system may include means for **determining whether a topic associated with a**

document changes over time; means for generating a score for the document based, at least in part, on the whether the topic associated with the document changes; and means for ranking the document with regard to at least one other document based, at least in part, on the score.

> *"A process to determine whether a documents content (topic) has changed and if that change requires a change to the documents score. This may effect at least one other document."*

BRIEF DESCRIPTION OF THE DRAWINGS

[0016] The accompanying drawings, which are incorporated in and constitute a part of this specification, illustrate an **embodiment of the invention** and, together with the description, **explain the invention**. In the drawings,

> *"Drawing are included to define the invention."*

[0017] FIG. 1 is a diagram of an **exemplary network** in which systems and methods consistent with the **principles of the invention may be implemented**;

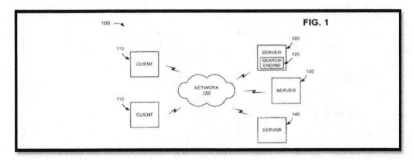

[0018] FIG. 2 is an exemplary diagram of a **client and/or server** of FIG. 1 according to an **implementation** consistent with the **principles of the invention**;

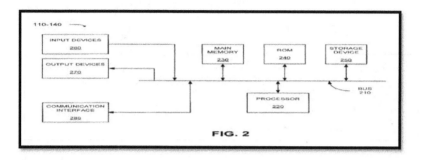

FIG. 2

[0019] FIG. 3 is an exemplary functional **block diagram of the search engine** of FIG. 1 according to an **implementation** consistent with the **principles of the invention**; and

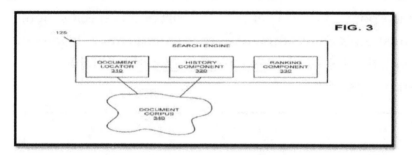

FIG. 3

[0020] FIGS. 4 is a **flowchart of exemplary processing for scoring documents** according to an **implementation** consistent with the **principles of the invention**.

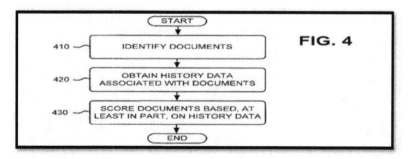

FIG. 4

DETAILED DESCRIPTION

[0021] The following **detailed description of the invention** refers to the accompanying drawings. The same reference numbers in different drawings may identify the same or similar elements. Also, the following detailed description **does not limit the invention**.

> *"Drawing included define the invention. The invention is not to be limited by these drawings."*

[0022] Systems and methods consistent with the principles of the invention may score documents using, for example, **history data associated with the documents**. The systems and methods may use these scores to **provide high quality search results**.

> *"The scores related to documents will be used to deliver high quality search results."*

[0023] A "document," as the term is used herein, is to be broadly interpreted to include any machine-readable and machine-storable work product. **A document may include an e-mail, a web site, a file, a combination of files, one or more files with embedded links to other files, a news group posting, a blog, a web advertisement, etc.** In the context of the Internet, a common document is a web page. Web pages often include textual information and may include embedded information (**such as meta information, images, hyperlinks, etc.**) and/or embedded instructions (such as **Javascript**, etc.). **A page may correspond to a document or a portion of a document**. Therefore, the words "**page**" and "**document**" **may be used interchangeably** in some cases. In other cases, a page may refer to a portion of a document, such as a sub-document. It may also be possible for a page to correspond to more than a single document.

> *"A document consists of all elements visual as well as behind the scenes like HTML code, images scripts, and any elements which are found on or used to make up the page. Anything within a document can be referred to or considered a web page. Neither necessarily mean a single page or single document. Interestingly, they also include the word "email" rather than "email address."*

[0024] In the description to follow, documents may be described as having links to other documents and/or links from other documents. **For example, when a document includes a link to another document, the link may be referred to as a "<u>forward link</u>." When a document includes a link from another document, the link may be referred to as a "<u>back link</u>." When the term "link" is used, it may refer to either a back link or a forward link**.

> *"The word 'link' can refer to either a forward link (outbound) or back link (inbound)."*

Exemplary Network Configuration

[0025] FIG. 1 is an **exemplary diagram of a network 100** in which systems and methods consistent with the principles of the invention may be implemented. **<u>Network 100 may include multiple clients 110 connected to multiple servers 120-140 via a network 150</u>**. Network 150 may include a local area network (LAN), a wide area network (WAN), a telephone network, such as the Public Switched Telephone

Network (PSTN), an intranet, the Internet, a memory device, another type of network, or a combination of networks. Two clients 110 and three servers 120-140 have been illustrated as connected to network 150 for simplicity. In practice, there may be more or fewer clients and servers. Also, in some instances, a client may perform the functions of a server and a server may perform the functions of a client.

> *"A hardware description and definition of the computer network for which the invention will run within between the users (clients) and the computers which store and use data exchanged."*

[0026] Clients 110 may include client entities. An entity may be defined as a device, such as a **wireless telephone, a personal computer, a personal digital assistant (PDA), a lap top, or another type of computation or communication device, a thread or process running on one of these devices, and/or an object executable by one of these device**. Servers 120-140 may include server entities that gather, process, search, and/or maintain documents in a manner consistent with the principles of the invention. Clients 110 and servers 120-140 may connect to network 150 via wired, wireless, and/or optical connections.

> *"Mostly a hardware description and definition of storage and various types of access devices. The network can be wireless or hardwired and could be any kind of device which is able to connect (phones, notebooks, person computers, tablets, whatever) and exchange, store or view data."*

[0027] In an implementation consistent with the principles of the invention, **server 120 may include a search engine 125 usable by clients 110. Server 120 may crawl a corpus of documents (e.g., web pages), index the documents, and store information associated with the documents in a repository of crawled documents.** Servers 130 and 140 may store or maintain documents that may be crawled by server 120. While servers 120-140 are shown as separate entities, it may be possible for one or more of servers 120-140 to perform one or more of the functions of another one or more of servers 120-140. **For example, it may be possible that two or more of servers 120-140 are implemented as a single server**. It may also be possible for a single one of servers 120-140 to be implemented as two or more separate (and possibly distributed) devices.

"Search engine 125 is the usable interface or portion of Google.com services which is available to users to run searches. Server 120 is the web crawling mechanism (spiders) and servers and 130 – 140 are likely used for date storage or are the datacenters which could have their own crawlers. So there could be any number of crawlers (spiders) and storage devices (data centers) being used."

Exemplary Client/Server Architecture

[0028] FIG. 2 **is an exemplary diagram of a client or server entity** (hereinafter called "**client/server entity**"), which may correspond to one or more of **clients 110 and servers 120-140**, according to an implementation consistent with the principles of the invention. The client/server entity may include a bus 210, a processor 220, a main memory 230, a read only memory (ROM) 240, a storage device 250, one or more input devices 260, one or more output devices 270, and a communication interface 280. Bus 210 may include one or more conductors that permit communication among the components of the client/server entity.

> *"Mostly a hardware description of storage, memory, recording and processing components."*

[0029] **Processor 220** may include one or more conventional processors or microprocessors that interpret and execute instructions. **Main memory 230** may include a random access memory (**RAM**) or another type of dynamic storage device that stores information and instructions for execution by processor 220. ROM 240 may include a conventional ROM device or another type of static storage device that stores static information and instructions for use by processor 220. Storage device 250 may include a magnetic and/or optical recording medium and its corresponding drive.

> *"Mostly a hardware description and definition of storage and various types of access devices."*

[0030] Input device(s) 260 may include one or more conventional mechanisms that permit an operator to input information to the **client/server entity, such as a keyboard, a mouse, a pen, voice recognition and/or biometric mechanisms,** etc. Output device(s) 270 may include one or more conventional mechanisms that output information to the operator, including a display, a printer, a speaker, etc. Communication interface 280 may include any transceiver-like mechanism that enables the client/server entity to communicate with other devices and/or systems. For example, communication interface 280 may include mechanisms for communicating with another device or system via a network, such as network 150.

> *"A hardware description of the network and various mechanisms of its data points. Also specifically mentions "biometrics" which could be voice recognition, fingerprint readers and/or face recognition (As being used by social networks like Facebook and now Google+)."*

[0031] As will be described in detail below, the client/server entity, consistent with the principles of the invention, perform certain searching-related operations. The client/server entity may perform these operations in response to **processor 220** executing software instructions contained in a computer-readable medium, such as **memory 230**. A computer-readable medium may be defined as one or more **physical or logical memory devices and/or carrier waves**.

> *"Mostly a hardware description of storage, memory, recording and processing components."*

[0032] The software instructions may be read into memory 230 from another computer-readable medium, such as data storage device 250, or from another device via communication interface 280. The software instructions contained in memory 230 may cause processor 220 to perform processes that will be described later. **Alternatively, hardwired circuitry may be used in place of or in combination with software instructions** to implement processes consistent with the principles of the invention.

Thus, implementations consistent with the principles of the invention are not limited to any specific combination of hardware circuitry and software.

> *"Mostly a hardware description and definition of storage and various types of access devices. The processes and hardware will be consistent with these methods but are not to be limited by them."*

Exemplary Search Engine

[0033] FIG. 3 is an **exemplary functional block diagram of search engine 125** according to an implementation consistent with the principles of the invention. Search engine 125 may include document locator 310, history component 320, and ranking component 330. As shown in FIG. 3, one or more of document locator 310 and history component 320 may connect to a document corpus 340. Document corpus 340 may include information associated with documents that were previously crawled, indexed, and stored, for example, in a database accessible by search engine 125. History data, as will be described in more detail below, may be associated with each of the documents in document corpus 340. **The history data may be stored in document corpus 340 or elsewhere.**

> *"Mostly a hardware description and definition of storage of historical data on documents. The access will be consistent with this concept but hardware for data is not to be limited by this."*

[0034] Document locator 310 may identify a set of documents whose contents match a user search query. **Document locator 310 may initially <u>locate documents from</u>**

document corpus 340 by comparing the terms in the user's search query to the documents in the corpus. In general, processes for indexing documents and searching the indexed collection to return a set of documents containing the searched terms are well known in the art. Accordingly, this functionality of document locator 310 will not be described further herein.

> *"A limited description of how the algorithm (The art of the invention) chooses a document from various documents in the corpus (storage area) which are likely many different machines which make up the different results seen when using or hitting various data centers."*

[0035] History component 320 may gather history data associated with the documents in document corpus 340. In implementations consistent with the principles of the invention, the **history data may include data relating to**: document **inception dates**; document **content updates/changes**; **query analysis**; **link-based criteria**; **anchor text** (e.g., the text in which a hyperlink is embedded, typically underlined or otherwise highlighted in a document); **traffic**; **user behavior**; **domain-related information**; **ranking history**; user maintained/generated data (e.g., **bookmarks**); unique **words**, **bigrams**, and **phrases in anchor text**; **linkage of independent peers**; and/or document **topics**. These different types of history data are described in additional detail below. In other implementations, the history data may include additional or different kinds of data.

> *"This is a description of all the things which are evaluated within the choosing and delivery process (algorithm) of returning a document. Items include: date the search engine first found the document, the content as well as its changes or frequency of change, its inbound and outbound link analysis, anchor text found within links which point to or from the document, traffic, user behavior, choosing or saving or bookmarking the document, keywords or key phrases, bounce rate, previous rankings, etc... "*

[0036] **Ranking component 330** may assign a ranking score (also called simply a "score" herein) to one or more documents in document corpus 340. **Ranking component 330 may assign the ranking scores prior to, independent of, or in connection with a search query**. When the documents are associated with a search query (e.g., identified as relevant to the search query), search engine 125 may **sort the documents based on the ranking score** and return the sorted set of documents to the client that submitted the search query. Consistent with aspects of the invention, the ranking score is a value that attempts to quantify the quality of the documents. In implementations consistent with the principles of the invention, the score is based, at least in part, on the history data from history component 320.

> *"This is a description of the component that ranks the documents based on their scores. This process determines what users see on Search Engine Results Pages (SERPS). The score of the documents are based on the historical data analysis of the documents as described in claim 0035."*

Exemplary History Data & Document Inception Date

[0037] According to an implementation consistent with the principles of the invention, a **document's inception date may be used to generate (or alter) a score associated with that document**. The term "date" is used broadly here and may, thus, include time and date measurements. As described below, there are several techniques that can be used to determine a document's inception date. **Some of these techniques are "biased" in the sense that they can be influenced by third parties desiring to improve the score associated with a document**. Other techniques are not biased. Any of these techniques, combinations of these techniques, or yet other techniques may be used to determine a document's inception date.

> *"A documents inception date is the first time the search engine discovers the document. This claim explains that a documents inception date is used as part of the scoring process and that an inception date for a document may change for appropriate reasons (for example if the document was completely updated) or manipulatively (with the intent only to improve its score) ."*

[0038] According to one implementation, the **inception date of a document may be determined from the date that search engine 125 first learns of or indexes the document**. Search engine 125 may discover the document through crawling, submission of the document (or a representation / summary thereof) to search engine 125 from an "outside" source, a combination of crawl or submission-based indexing techniques, or in other ways. Alternatively, the inception date of a **document may be determined from the date that search engine 125 first discovers a link to the document.**

[0039] According to another implementation, the **date that a domain** with which a document **is registered** may be used as an indication of the inception date of the document. According to yet another implementation, **the first time that a document is referenced in another document**, such as a news article, newsgroup, mailing list, or a combination of one or more such documents, may be used to infer an inception date of the document. According to a further implementation, the date that a document includes at least a threshold number of pages may be used as an indication of the inception date of the document. According to another implementation, the **inception date of a document may be equal to a time stamp associated with the document by the server hosting the document**. Other techniques, not specifically mentioned herein, or combinations of techniques could be used to determine or infer a document's inception date.

[0040] **Search engine 125 may use the <u>inception date of a document for scoring</u> of the document**. For example, it may be assumed that a document with a fairly recent inception date will not have a significant number of links from other documents (i.e., back links). **For existing <u>link-based scoring techniques</u> that score based on the number of links to/from a document, this recent document may be scored lower than an older document that has a larger number of links (e.g., back links)**. When the inception date of the documents are considered, however, the **<u>scores of the documents may be modified (either positively or negatively) based on the documents' inception dates</u>**.

> *"A documents inception date can be used to score a document specifically in evaluating how many links are pointing to it, whereas a new document with a few new links could be better than an old document which had lots of links, but no recent links when considering their inception dates ."*

[0041] Consider the example of a document with an inception date of yesterday that is **<u>referenced by 10 back links</u>**. This document may be scored higher by search engine 125 than a document with an inception date of 10 years ago that is **<u>referenced by 100 back links</u>** because the rate of link growth for the former is relatively higher than the latter. While a spiky rate of **<u>growth in the number of back links may be a factor</u>** used by search engine 125 to score documents, it may also signal an attempt to spam search engine 125. Accordingly, in this situation, search engine 125 **may actually lower the score of a document**(s) to **<u>reduce the effect of spamming</u>**.

> *"The speed in which links are acquired (based on a documents inception date), can have both positive and negative effects on documents whereas if a document seems to be acquiring links too quickly, it could be determined as spam which would then lower the documents score and rankings based on how many links the document has acquired since its inception date."*

[0042] Thus, according to an implementation consistent with the principles of the invention, **search engine 125 may use the inception date of a document to determine a rate at which links to the document are created** (e.g., as an average per unit time based on the number of links created since the inception date or some window in that period). This rate can then be used to score the document, for example, **giving more weight to documents to which links are generated more often**.

> *"A process at which a documents inception date is used along with a measurement to determine the rate at which links are acquired based on a timeframe from inception giving more weight and/or a higher score to documents which generate and acquire links more quickly or more often."*

[0043] In one implementation, search engine 125 may modify the link-based score of a document as follows: **H=L/log(F+2)**, where H may refer to the history-adjusted link score, L may refer to the link score given to the document, which can be derived using any known link **scoring technique** (e.g., the scoring technique described in U.S. Pat. No. 6,285,999) that assigns a score to a document based on links to/from the document, and F may refer to elapsed time measured from the inception date associated with the document (or a window within this period).

> *"A process that adjusts an overall link score (L – Link Score) by examining the freshness of the link (F – Elapsed Time from the Inception Date) as well as all measurable and historical information (H – History-Adjusted Link Score) from the document in which the link is pointing to or where the link is pointing from (Includes reference to a previous patent for PageRank U.S. Pat. No. 6,285,999 "Method for Node Ranking in a Linked Database – by Lawrence Page)."*

[0044] For some queries, **older documents may be more favorable than newer ones**. As a result, it may be beneficial to adjust the score of a document based on the difference (in age) from the average age of the result set. In other words, search engine 125 may determine the age of each of the documents in a result set (e.g., **using their inception dates**), determine the average age of the documents, and modify the scores of the documents (either positively or negatively) based on a difference between the documents' age and the average age.

> *"In some instances, older documents may be better than newer ones. Using the inception dates, an average may be taken among multiple documents and used to assign scores based on age."*

[0045] In summary, search engine 125 **may generate (or alter) a score** associated with a document based, at least in part, on information relating to the **inception date of the document**.

> *"Using the inception date, a process may be used to adjust the score (either positively or negatively) of a document or set of documents based on the documents age."*

Content Updates/Changes

[0046] According to an implementation consistent with the principles of the invention, information relating to a **manner in which a document's content changes over time may be used to generate (or alter) a score associated with that document**. For example, a document whose content is edited often may be scored differently than a document whose content remains static over time. Also, a document having a relatively large amount of its content updated over time might be scored differently than a document having a relatively small amount of its content updated over time.

> *"The amount of change to a document and the frequency of that change is used to alter the score of a document (either positively or negatively). More than likely, significant and frequent changes and the freshening up of documents is positive."*

[0047] In one implementation, search engine 125 may generate a content update score **(U)** as follows: **U=f(UF,UA),** where f may refer to a function, such as a sum or weighted sum, **UF** may refer to an **update frequency score** that represents how often a document (or page) is updated, and **UA** may refer to an **update amount score** that represents how much the document (or page) has changed over time. **UF** may be determined in a number of ways, including as an average time between updates, the number of updates in a given time period, etc.

> *"The 'frequency of content change' (UF) and the 'amount of content change' (UA) is used to determine 'overall content score' (U), whereas, lots of large frequent changes are likely positive."*

[0048] UA may also be determined as a function of one or more factors, such as **the number of "new" or unique pages associated with a document over a period of time**. Another factor might include the ratio of the number of new or unique pages associated with a document over a period of time versus the total number of pages associated with that document. <u>**Yet another factor may include the amount that the document is updated over one or more periods of time**</u> (e.g., n % of a document's visible content may change over a period t (e.g., last m months)), which might be an average value. A further factor might include the amount that the document (or page) has changed in one or more periods of time (e.g., within the last x days).

> *"The amount of content (UA) which changes over time and the frequency of those changes as well as associated documents are used to determine and influence the total amount of update score)."*

[0049] According to one exemplary implementation, UA may be determined as a function of differently weighted portions of document content. For instance, **content deemed to be unimportant if updated/changed**, such as Javascript, comments, advertisements, navigational elements, boilerplate material, or date/time tags, <u>**may be given relatively little weight or even ignored altogether**</u>

when determining UA. On the other hand, **content deemed to be important if updated/changed** (e.g., more often, more recently, more extensively, etc.), such as the title or anchor text associated with the forward links, **could be given more weight** than changes to other content **when determining UA**.

> *"The types of changes to a page are significant whereas minor changes to internal code and non-visible items or advertisements are not changes of true substance to the content or what the reader or visitors will find of value and do not matter as much so significant content changes are more relevant. Updating dead outbound links suggest editorial discretion and are likely positive."*

[0050] **UF and UA may be used in other ways to influence the score assigned to a document**. For example, the **rate of change** in a current time period can be compared to the rate of change in another (e.g., previous) time period to determine whether there is an **acceleration or deceleration trend**. Documents for which there is an increase in the rate of change might be scored higher than those documents for which there is a steady rate of change, even if that rate of change is relatively high. The **amount of change may also be a factor in this scoring**. For example, documents for which there is an **increase in the rate of change** when that amount of change is greater than some threshold might be scored higher than those documents for which there is a steady rate of change or an amount of change is less than the threshold.

> *"Documents which are found to have an increasing 'frequency of content change' (UF) as well as an increasing 'amount of content change' (UA) may be scored higher even if their previous frequency (UF) and amount (UA) was already relatively high."*

[0051] In some situations, data storage resources may be insufficient to store the documents when monitoring the documents for content changes. In this case, search engine 125 may store representations of the documents and monitor these representations for changes. For example, **search engine 125 may store "signatures" of documents instead of the (entire) documents** themselves to detect changes to document content. In this case, search engine 125 may store a term vector for a document (or page) and monitor it for relatively large changes. According to another implementation, search engine 125 may store and monitor a relatively small portion (e.g., a few terms) of the documents that are determined to be important or the most frequently occurring (excluding "stop words").

> *"In some instances, due to storage abilities or inabilities, a vector image, limited keyword data, signature or a partial document may be stored rather than an entire copy of a document."*

[0052] According to yet another implementation, **search engine 125 may store a summary or other representation of a document and monitor this information for changes**. According to a further implementation, search engine 125 may generate a similarity hash (which may be used to detect near-duplication of a document) for the document and monitor it for changes. A change in a similarity hash may be considered to indicate a relatively large change in its associated document. In other implementations, yet other techniques may be used to monitor documents for changes. In situations where adequate data storage resources exist, the full documents may be stored and used to determine changes rather than some representation of the documents.

> *"In some instances a summary of a document or other techniques may be used to store limited information only to monitor changes to documents to determine or detect duplicate content."*

[0053] For some queries, documents with content that has not recently changed may be more favorable than documents with content that has recently changed. As a result, it may be beneficial to adjust the score of a document based on the difference from the average date-of-change of the result set. In other words, **search engine 125 may determine a date when the content of each of the documents in a result set last changed, <u>determine the average date of change for the documents</u>, and modify the scores of the documents** (either positively or negatively) based on a difference between the documents' date-of-change and the average date-of-change.

> *"In some instances documents which have not changed may be better when there are multiple similar documents. The average date of change (or no change) may be used to modify scores."*

[0054] In summary, **search engine 125 may generate (or alter) a score associated with a document based, at least in part, on information <u>relating to a manner in which the document's content changes over time</u>**. For very large documents that include content belonging to multiple individuals or organizations, the score may correspond to each of the sub-documents (i.e., that content belonging to or updated by a single individual or organization).

> *"In a case where documents, sections of documents, or related subdocuments change, the score which is assigned may be assigned only to certain sections or subdocuments, and not to the entire document. Sections of pages which changed recently may be better than sections with no change."*

Query Analysis

[0055] According to an implementation consistent with the principles of the invention, one or more **query-based factors may be used to generate (or alter) a score associated with a document**. For example, one query-based factor may relate to the extent to which a document is selected over time when the **document is included in a set of search results**. In this case, search engine 125 might score documents selected relatively more often/increasingly by users higher than other documents.

> *"This process evaluates search habits, bounce-rates, time on site, etc. to determine the quality of documents within search results and alter the scores (or rank the documents) accordingly."*

[0056] Another query-based factor may relate to the occurrence of certain search terms appearing in queries over time. A particular set of search terms may increasingly appear in queries over a period of time. **For example, terms relating to a "hot" topic that is gaining/has gained** popularity or a breaking news event would conceivably appear frequently over a period of time. In this case, search engine 125 may score documents associated with these search terms (or queries) higher than documents not associated with these terms.

> *"This process measures for a 'buzz ' factor and will evaluate search queries over time. If a particular term begins to be searched more frequently, documents which contain the terms will begin to rank higher as people are looking for this information more ."*

[0057] A further query-based factor may relate to a change over time in the number of search results generated by similar queries. A **significant increase in the number of search results** generated by similar queries, for example, **might indicate a hot topic or breaking news** and cause search engine 125 to **increase the scores of documents** related to such queries.

> *"Again, this process is looking for a 'buzz ' factor and will evaluate search queries over time whereas if a particular term begins to be searched more frequently, documents which contain the term will be scored more positively as people are obviously looking for this*

[0058] Another query-based factor may relate to queries that remain relatively constant over time but lead to results that change over time. For example, a query relating to "world series champion" **leads to search results that change over time** (e.g., documents relating to a particular team dominate search results in a given year or time of year). This change can be monitored and used to score documents accordingly.

> *"This process recognizes that queries could stay the same throughout a time period but at certain points the answers could actually change depending on events like a World Series Championship, so search habits and user selected documents are monitored to decipher these type changes. "*

[0059] Yet another query-based factor might relate to the "staleness" of documents returned as search results. The **staleness of a document** may be **based** on factors, such as **document creation date, anchor growth, traffic, content change, forward/back link growth, etc.** For some queries, recent documents are very important (e.g., if searching for Frequently Asked Questions (FAQ) files, the most recent version would be highly desirable). Search engine 125 may learn which queries recent changes are most important for by analyzing which documents in search results are selected by users. More specifically, **search engine 125 may consider how often users favor a more recent document that is ranked lower than an older document in the search results**. Additionally, if over time a particular document is included in mostly topical queries (e.g.,. "World Series Champions") versus more specific queries (e.g., "New York Yankees"), then this query-based factor--by itself or with others mentioned herein--may be used to **lower a score for a document that appears to be stale**.

> *"Using query based data as well as the monitoring of how those results are used could signal or indicate certain documents are better than others regardless of inception dates, backlinks, etc."*

[0060] **In some situations, a stale document may be considered more favorable than more recent documents.**

As a result, search engine 125 may consider the extent to which a document is selected over time when generating a score for the document. For example, **if** for a given query, **users over time tend to select a lower ranked, relatively stale, document over a higher ranked, relatively recent document**, this may be used by search engine 125 as an indication to **adjust a score of the stale document**.

> *"Using query based data as well as the monitoring of how those results are used is likely to affect (either positively or negatively) how a document is scored and ranked within search results."*

[0061] Yet another query-based factor may relate to the extent to which a document appears in results for different queries. In other words, the **entropy of queries** for one or more documents **may be monitored** and used as a basis for scoring. For example, if a particular document appears as a hit for a discordant set of queries, this may (though not necessarily) be considered a **signal that the document is spam**, in which case search engine 125 **may score the document relatively lower**.

> *"If many different queries generate a document to appear and that document (through monitoring the results and user habits) doesn't seem relevant to those queries (lots of bounces), the document will likely be deemed a poor result and/or may be scored lower based*

[0062] In summary, **search engine 125 may generate (or alter) a score associated with a document based, at least in part, on one or more query-based factors**.

Link-Based Criteria

[0063] According to an implementation consistent with the principles of the invention, one or more **link-based factors may be used to generate (or alter) a score associated with a document**. In one implementation, the link-based factors **may relate to the dates that new links appear to a document and that existing links disappear**. The appearance date of a link may be the first date that search engine 125 finds the link or the date of the document that contains the link (e.g., the date that the document was found with the link or the date that it was last updated). The disappearance date of a link may be the first date that the document containing the link either dropped the link or disappeared itself.

[0064] These dates may be determined by search engine 125 during a crawl or index update operation. Using this date as a reference, search engine 125 may then **monitor the time-varying behavior of links to the document, such as when links appear or disappear**, the **rate at which links appear or disappear over time, how many links appear or disappear during a given time period, whether there is trend toward appearance of new links versus disappearance of existing links to the document**, etc.

> *"This process examines and measures the behavior (both link growth and link decline) over time (how many links appear or disappear) to decipher and identify a trend either up or down."*

[0065] Using the time-varying behavior of links to (and/or from) a document, search engine 125 may score the document accordingly. For example, **a downward trend in the number or rate of new links** (e.g., based on a comparison of the number or rate of new links in a recent time period versus an older time period) over time **could signal** to search engine 125 **that a document is stale**, in which case search engine 125 **may decrease the document's score. Conversely, an upward trend may signal a "fresh" document** (e.g., a document whose content is fresh--recently created or updated) that might be considered more relevant, depending on the particular situation and implementation.

> *"A downward trend of new links lowers a score; an upward trend raises a score of a document."*

[0066] By **analyzing the change in the number or rate of increase/decrease of back links** to a document (or page) over time, search engine 125 may derive a **valuable signal of how fresh the document is**. For example, if such analysis is reflected by a curve that is dropping off, this may signal that the document may be stale (e.g., no longer updated, diminished in importance, **superseded by another document**, etc.).

> *"By monitoring link behavior (increase verses decrease), scores can be determined to identify the popularity of documents; documents which have been superseded by other (better) documents."*

[0067] According to one implementation, the **analysis may depend on the number of new links to a document**. For example, search engine 125 may **monitor the number of new links** to a document in the last n days compared to the number of new links since the document was first found. Alternatively, search engine 125 may determine the oldest age of the most recent y % of links compared to the age of the first link found.

> *"By monitoring link behavior, the frequency of new links can be identified and compared over a period of time since the first links were found to a document and identify a spike or decline."*

[0068] For the purpose of illustration, consider y=10 and two documents (web sites in this example) that were both first found 100 days ago. **For the first site, 10% of the links were found less than 10 days ago, while for the second site 0% of the links were found less than 10 days ago (in other words, they were all found earlier). In this case, the metric results in 0.1 for site A and 0 for site B.** The metric may be scaled appropriately. In another exemplary implementation, the metric may be modified by performing a relatively more detailed analysis of the distribution of link dates. For example, models may be built that predict if a particular distribution signifies a particular type of site (e.g., a site that is no longer updated, increasing or decreasing in popularity, superseded, etc.).

> *"Again, by monitoring link behavior, the frequency of new links can be identified and compared over a period of time since the first links were found to a document and identify a spike or decline. Example: Site A could have more links than Site B overall, but Site B may still score higher than Site A in the event Site B has more links which have been acquired recently."*

[0069] According to another implementation, the **analysis may depend on weights assigned to the links**. In this case, each link may be **weighted by a function that increases with the freshness of the link**. The freshness of a link may be determined by the date of appearance/ change of the link, the date of appearance / change of anchor text associated with the link, date of appearance / change of the document containing the link. The date of appearance / change of the document containing a link may be a better indicator of the freshness of the link based on the theory that a good link may go unchanged when a document gets updated if it is still relevant and good. **In order to not update every link's freshness from a minor edit of a tiny unrelated part of a document, each updated document may be tested for significant changes (e.g., changes to a large portion of the document or changes to many different portions of the document) and a link's freshness may be updated (or not updated) accordingly.**

> *"A process in which there is an assigning of a freshness value to a link by looking at when the link first appeared or was updated. This process will also examine the document to which contains the link thoroughly to identify whether a change to the link or just the document is a minor or major change, whether or not the section of the document was relevant to the link and whether or not the links freshness value should be changed according to the significance of the modification to the overall document. Example, a link may or may not change, but depending on the significance of the change to the document, in particular, where the change was made within the document, (was the change even close to the link) the links may or may not be scored differently."*

[0070] **Links may be weighted in other ways.** For example, **links may be <u>weighted</u> based on <u>how much the documents containing the links are trusted</u>** (e.g., government documents can be given high trust). **Links may also, or alternatively, be <u>weighted</u> based on how authoritative the documents containing the links are** (e.g., authoritative documents may be determined in a manner similar to that described in **<u>U.S. Pat. No. 6,285,999</u>**). Links may also, or alternatively, be weighted based on the freshness of the documents containing the links using some other features to establish freshness (e.g., a document that is updated frequently (e.g., the Yahoo home page) suddenly drops a link to a document).

> *"Some documents rank better solely based on their author or where they are published from. The authority of a document (Patent: Method for node ranking in a linked database "PageRank") assigns a trust level on authoritative sources and/or publishers while freshness is also measured."*

[0071] Search engine 125 may raise or lower the score of a document to which there are links as a function of the **sum of the weights of the links pointing to it**. This technique may be employed recursively. For example, assume that a document S is 2 years olds. **Document S may be considered fresh if n % of the links to S are fresh or if the documents containing forward links to S are considered fresh**. The latter can be checked by using the creation date of the document and applying this technique recursively.

> *"Freshness, relevance and weight of links as well as the sources of those links are important. For instance, if Site A has links to Site B, the amount of benefit Site B receives is based, at least in part, by the weight, relevance and freshness of the links which point to Site A."*

[0072] According to yet another technique, the **analysis may depend on an age distribution associated with the links pointing to a document**. In other words, the dates that the links to a document were created may be determined and input to a function that determines the age distribution. It may be assumed that the **age distribution** of a **stale document will be very different from the age distribution of a fresh document**. Search engine 125 may then score documents based, at least in part, on the age distributions associated with the documents.

> *"Freshness, relevance and weight of link sources are taken into account. For Example, if Site A has links to Site B, the age distribution of the links (which could be fresh or stale) pointing to Site A can make a difference in the amount of benefit Site B will receive from the links pointing from Site A."*

[0073] **The dates that links appear can also be used to detect "spam,"** where owners of documents or their colleagues create links to their own document for the purpose of boosting the score assigned by a search engine. A typical, **"legitimate" document attracts back links slowly**. A **large spike in the quantity of back links may signal a topical phenomenon** (e.g., the CDC web site may develop many links quickly after an outbreak, such as SARS), **or signal attempts to spam a search engine** (to obtain a higher ranking and, thus, better placement in search results) by exchanging links, **purchasing links, or gaining links from documents without editorial discretion on making links**. Examples of documents that give links without editorial discretion include guest books, referrer logs, and "free for all" pages that let anyone add a link to a document.

> *"Gaining too many inbound links too quickly could signal either a "hot topic" or a spam attempt. A process is used to evaluate links which are acquired quickly or sites which seem to display little editorial discretion with links (unrelated outbound links) to evaluate possible spam attempts."*

[0074] According to a further implementation, the **analysis may depend on the date that links disappear**. The disappearance of many links can mean that the document to which these links point is stale (e.g., no longer being updated or has been superseded by another document). For example, search engine 125 may **monitor the date at which one or more links to a document disappear**, the number of links that disappear in a given window of time, or some other time-varying decrease in the number of links (or links/updates to the documents containing such links) to a document to identify documents that may be **considered stale**. **Once a document has been determined to be stale, the links contained in that document may be discounted or ignored by search engine 125 when determining scores for documents pointed to by the links.**

> *"Losing links to a document quickly is a signal that a document is no longer relevant, is stale or has been superseded by another document. Once a document has been deemed of lesser value, the links within the stale document lose their value and credibility for sources in which they reference."*

[0075] According to another implementation, **the analysis may depend, not only on the age of the links** to a document, **but also on the dynamic-ness of the links**. As such, search engine 125 may weight documents that have a different featured link each day, despite having a very fresh link, differently (e.g., lower) than documents that are consistently updated and **consistently link to a given target document**. In one exemplary implementation, search engine 125 may generate a score for a document based on the scores of the documents with links to the document for all versions of the documents within a window of time. Another version of this may factor a discount/decay into the integration based on the major update times of the document.

> *"A link which remains on a page which is updated significantly and often will continually freshen its value as it is an indication that despite frequent and significant changes, these links remain. In addition, if a link remains on an unchanged page, and that page is not considered fresh either through changes to its content or continual inbound links, the value of that link will diminish."*

[0076] In summary, search engine 125 may **generate (or alter) a score** associated with a document **based**, at least in part, **on** one **or more link-based factors**.

> *"Various link based factors will alter (either positively or negatively) the value of a document."*

Anchor Text

[0077] According to an implementation consistent with the principles of the invention, information relating to a **manner in which anchor text changes over time may be used to generate (or alter) a score associated with a document**. For example, changes over time in anchor text associated with links to a document may be used as an indication that there has been an update or even a change of focus in the document.

> *"If and when the anchor text of a link changes, there will be an expectation that there is a valid reason why that links anchor text would have changed. For example, a change in anchor text should be accompanied by a change in the document it points to (the target document)."*

[0078] Alternatively, if the **content of a document changes such that it differs significantly from the anchor text associated with its back links**, then the domain associated with the document may have **changed significantly (completely)** from a previous incarnation. This may occur when a **domain expires and a different party purchases the domain**. Because anchor text is often considered to be part of the document to which its associated link points, the domain may show up in search results for queries that are no longer on topic. This is an undesirable result.

> *"If a document has many backlinks pointing to it but suddenly changes in topic significantly, it is very likely that the backlinks to the document will no longer be counted. This is an indication that purchasing a domain name and changing its focus will not harness the full backlink benefits. Furthermore, if at any time a document changes significantly, it may lose the value being applied to it from the backlinks if the anchor text being used is no longer relevant to the documents*

[0079] One way to address this problem is to **estimate the date that a domain changed its focus**. This may be done by determining a date when the text of a document changes significantly or when the text of the anchor text changes significantly. **All links and/or anchor text prior to that date may then be ignored or discounted**.

> *"If a document has many backlinks pointing to it but the document (or domain name) suddenly changes in topic or focus significantly it is very likely that all backlinks identified to have existed before the date of the significant change will diminish in value and those backlinks (since they are no longer relevant) will no longer be counted in calculating the importance of the document."*

[0080] The **freshness of anchor text may also be used as a factor in scoring documents**. The freshness of an anchor text may be determined, for example, by the date of appearance/change of the anchor text, the **date of appearance/change of the link** associated with the anchor text, and/or the date of appearance/change of the document to which the associated link points. The date of appearance/change of the document pointed to by the link may be a good indicator of the freshness of the anchor text based on the theory that good anchor text may go unchanged when a document gets updated if it is still relevant and good. In order to not update an anchor text's freshness from a minor edit of a tiny unrelated part of a document, each updated document may be tested for significant changes (e.g., changes to a large portion of the document or changes to many different portions of the document) and an anchor text's freshness may be updated (or not updated) accordingly.

> *"A process in which there is an assigning of a freshness value to an anchor text of a link by looking at when the link first appeared with its original anchor text and when it was updated. This process will also examine the document to which the link points to thoroughly to identify whether a change to the document is a minor or major change, whether or not the section of the document was relevant to the link and whether or not the links anchor text would be considered fresh based on the change. This process will closely look to see if a change in the anchor text of the link is accompanied by a related change in the document it points to (the target document)."*

[0081] In summary, search engine 125 **may generate (or alter) a score associated** with a document based, at least in part, on information relating to a manner in which anchor text changes over time.

> *"A score for a link is based, at least in part, by its anchor text and may be altered (either positively or negatively) in the event the anchor text changes depending on the significance and determined reasoning of the change to the anchor text. Changing anchor text to documents does matter."*

Traffic

[0082] According to an implementation consistent with the principles of the invention, information relating to traffic associated with a document over time may be used to generate (or alter) a score associated with the document. For example, search engine 125 may **monitor the time-varying characteristics of traffic to, or other "use" of, a document by one or more users**. A large reduction in traffic may indicate that a document may be stale (e.g., no longer be updated or may be superseded by another document).

> *"Traffic trends monitored over time will alter (either positively or negatively) the score of a document. For example, significant reductions in traffic when measured over a period of time would indicate that a document has become stale or is now less important than it was previously."*

[0083] In one implementation, search engine 125 may compare the average traffic for a document over the last j days (e.g., where j=30) to the average traffic during the month where the document received the most traffic, optionally adjusted for seasonal changes, or during the last k days (e.g., where k=365). Optionally, search engine 125 may **identify repeating traffic patterns or perhaps a change in traffic patterns over time**. It may be discovered that there are periods when a document is more or less popular (i.e., has more or less traffic), such as during the summer months, on weekends, or during some other seasonal time period. By identifying repeating traffic patterns or changes in traffic patterns, search engine 125 may appropriately adjust its scoring of the document during and outside of these periods.

> *"Sites having characteristics which indicate traffic spikes only during repeated timeframes such as seasonal or certain months (when monitored and consistent over time) are treated differently near or around those time periods as traffic evidence indicates the documents are more relevant in, near or around those timeframes. Ex: If traffic is high during J (month) each time it is measured over a period of K (year), traffic is more relevant near/around J each K."*

[0084] Additionally, or alternatively, search engine 125 may monitor time-varying characteristics relating to "**advertising traffic**" for a particular document. For example, search engine 125 may monitor one or a combination of the following factors: (1) **the extent to and rate at which advertisements are presented** or updated by a given document over time; (2) the **quality of the advertisers** (e.g., a document whose advertisements refer/link to documents known to search engine 125 over time to have relatively high traffic and trust, such as amazon.com, may be given relatively more weight than those documents whose advertisements refer to low traffic/untrustworthy documents, such as a pornographic site); and (3) **the extent to which the advertisements generate user traffic** to the documents to which they relate (e.g., their click-through rate). Search engine 125 may use these time-varying characteristics relating to advertising traffic to score the document.

> *"A process which examines outbound links to identify "advertising traffic". These advertising links can be measured for their trust, effectiveness and the quality of the advertiser. The documents to which they point to will be measured using time-varying traffic trends to score the document."*

[0085] In summary, search engine 125 **may generate (or alter) a** <u>score</u> **associated with a document** <u>based</u>, at least in part, **on information relating to traffic** associated with the document over time.

> *"Traffic trends to and from a document can be used to generate or alter a score to a document."*

User Behavior

[0086] According to an implementation consistent with the principles of the invention, information corresponding to individual or aggregate user **<u>behavior</u>** relating to a document over time may be **<u>used to generate (or alter) a score associated with the document</u>**. For example, search engine 125 may monitor the number of times that a document is selected from a set of search results and/or the amount of time one or more users spend accessing the document. Search engine 125 may then score the document based, at least in part, on this information.

> *"Bounce rate is measured to generate or alter a score to both a document and search results."*

[0087] If a document is returned for a certain query and over time, or within a given time window, **<u>users spend either more or less time on average on the document</u>** given the same or similar query, then this may be used as an indication that the document is fresh or stale, respectively. For example, assume that the query "Riverview swimming schedule" returns a document with the title "Riverview Swimming Schedule." Assume further that users used to spend 30 seconds accessing it, but now **every user that selects the document only spends a few seconds accessing it**. Search engine 125 may use this information to determine that the document is stale (i.e., contains an outdated swimming schedule) and score the document accordingly.

> *"When a document and its users behavior is measured over time, and the amount of time a user spends on that document decreases or the bounce rate increases, this will be used to determine that the document is now stale or out of date and the score for the document should decrease."*

[0088] In summary, search engine 125 may **generate (or alter) a score** associated with a document based, at least in part, on information corresponding to individual or aggregate **user behavior** relating to the document over time.

> *"User behavior will be used to alter a score of a document (either positively or negatively) ."*

Domain-Related Information

[0089] According to an implementation consistent with the principles of the invention, information relating to a **domain associated with a document may be used to generate (or alter) a score** associated with the document. For example, search engine 125 may monitor information relating to how a document is hosted within a computer network (e.g., the Internet, an intranet or other network or database of documents) and use this information to score the document.

> *"Domain names, name servers and IP addresses call all be used to alter a documents score."*

[0090] Individuals who attempt to deceive (**spam**) search engines often use throwaway or "doorway" domains and attempt to obtain as much traffic as possible before being caught. **Information regarding the legitimacy of the domains may be used** by search engine 125 **when scoring** the documents associated with these domains.

> *"Domain names can be used to determine the legitimacy of a web site. The speculation on through-away $1.99 .info domain registrations was correct."*

[0091] Certain signals may be used to distinguish between illegitimate and legitimate domains. For example, domains can be renewed up to a period of 10 years. Valuable **(legitimate) domains are often paid for several years in advance**, while doorway (illegitimate) domains rarely are used for more than a year. Therefore, the date when a domain expires in the future can be used as a factor in predicting the legitimacy of a domain and, thus, the documents associated therewith.

> *"Indication that domain registration length can be used to determine the legitimacy of a site. Domains registered for ten (10) years are far more likely to be more legitimate than one registered for only one (1) or two (2) years (the minimum registration length)."*

[0092] Also, or alternatively, the domain name server **(DNS) record for a domain may be monitored to predict whether a domain is legitimate**. The DNS record contains details of who registered the domain, administrative and technical addresses, and the addresses of name servers (i.e., servers that resolve the domain name into an IP address). By analyzing this data over time for a domain, illegitimate domains may be identified. **For instance, search engine 125 may monitor whether physically correct address information exists over a period of time, whether contact information for the domain changes relatively often, whether there is a relatively high number of changes between different name servers and hosting companies, etc.** In one implementation, a list of known-bad contact information, name servers, and/or IP addresses may be identified, stored, and used in predicting the legitimacy of a domain and, thus, the documents associated therewith.

> *"Domain name should be registered with accurate and complete information that does not change often. This process may try to establish a relation to the address of a web site with maps or other local services and monitor WhoIs data to find addresses on registrants and try to match them with other references to that business using sites like yellow pages, super pages or other local trusted directories to establish a genuine location as geographic searches become more important and legitimate businesses usually have findable and verifiable corresponding physical addresses. This process likely already relies on the Addresses Verification Process - PIN Number Postcard Mailer."*

[0093] Also, or alternatively, the age, or other information, regarding a name server associated with a domain may be used to predict the legitimacy of the domain. **A "good" name server may have a mix of different domains from different registrars and have a history of hosting those domains,** while a "bad" name server might host mainly pornography or doorway domains, domains with commercial words (a common indicator of spam), or primarily bulk domains from a single registrar, or might be brand new**. The newness of a name server might not automatically be a negative factor in determining the legitimacy of the associated domain, but in combination with other factors, such as ones described herein, it could be.

> *"Hosting web sites on established name servers is more trusted. Hosting web sites on name servers which do not allow low quality sites or many sites which have been identified as spam is preferred. maintaining a dedicated IP address which is not shared and used for 1 site only is also preferred. Example, a name server (NS1.NAMESERVER.COM) may host all different things, or all similar things.*

[0094] In summary, search engine 125 **may generate (or alter) a <u>score</u> associated with a document based, at least in part, on information <u>relating to a legitimacy of a domain</u> associated with the document.**

> *"A domain name history, age, network relationship, ownership and other available information in relation to a domain name can alter (either positively or negatively) the score of a web site."*

Ranking History

[0095] According to an implementation consistent with the principles of the invention, information relating to **<u>prior rankings of a document may be used to generate (or alter) a score associated with the document</u>**. For example, search engine 125 may monitor the time-varying ranking of a document in response to search queries provided to search engine 125. Search engine 125 may determine that a document that jumps in rankings across many queries might be a topical document or it could signal an attempt to spam search engine 125.

> *"A document which experiences a spike or jump in rankings for a particular term or group of terms when monitored over a period of time will be examined closely to identify whether it is moving due to a spam attempt or is related to a trending topic, then alter (either positively or negatively) its score."*

[0096] Thus, the quantity or **rate that a document moves in rankings over a period of time might be used to influence future scores assigned to that document**. In one implementation, for each set of search results, a document may be weighted according to its position in the top N search results. For N=30, one example function might **be [((N+1)-SLOT)/N].sup.4.** In this case, a top result may receive a score of 1.0, down to a score near 0 for the Nth result.

> *"A spike in rankings for a particular document can be monitored over a period of time to identify how many places it moves and can influence future scores assigned to the document. How much a site moves within a period of time is measured and alter (either positively or negatively) its score."*

[0097] A query set (e.g., of commercial queries) can be repeated, and documents that gained more than M % in the rankings may be flagged or the percentage growth in ranking may be used as a signal in determining scores for the documents. For example, search engine 125 may **determine that a query is likely commercial** if the average (median) score of the top results is relatively high and there is a significant amount of change in the top results from month to month. Search engine 125 may also monitor churn as an indication of a commercial query. For commercial queries, **the likelihood of spam is higher**, so search engine 125 **may treat documents associated therewith accordingly.**

> *"Terms identified as highly competitive or related to business services and commercial services which shift around often are treated with more scrutiny."*

[0098] In addition to history of positions (or rankings) of documents for a given query, search engine 125 **may monitor** (on a page, host, document, and/or domain basis) one or more other factors, such as **the number of queries for which, and the rate at which (increasing/decreasing), a document is selected as a search result over time;** seasonality, burstiness, and other patterns over time that a document is selected as a search result; and/or changes in scores over time for a URL-query pair.

> *"Documents which display characteristics which indicate they are being chosen more frequently during certain timeframes such certain months of a year are treated differently near or around those time periods. This may affect not only one document but an entire given URL (domain)."*

[0099] In addition, or alternatively, search engine 125 **may monitor a number of document (e.g., URL) independent query-based criteria over time**. For example, search engine 125 may monitor the average score among a top set of results generated in response to a given query or set of queries and adjust the score of that set of results and/or other results generated in response to the given query or set of queries. Moreover, search engine 125 may monitor the number of results generated for a particular query or set of queries over time. If search engine 125 determines that the number of results increases or that there is a change in the rate of increase (e.g., such an increase may be an indication of a "**hot topic" or other phenomenon**), **search engine 125 may score those results higher in the future**.

> *"Documents identified as related to trending or hot topics can be displayed differently (likely higher in the results) due to a 'buzz' factor indicating a significant interest in this information. These are also measurements of not only topic, but the URL's users tend to choose more often."*

[0100] In addition, or alternatively, search engine 125 may monitor the ranks of documents over time to detect sudden spikes in the ranks of the documents. **A spike may indicate either a topical phenomenon (e.g., a hot topic) or an attempt to spam search engine 125 by, for example, trading or purchasing links.** Search engine 125 may take measures to prevent spam attempts by, for example, employing hysteresis to **allow a rank to grow at a certain rate**. In another implementation, the rank for a **given document may be allowed a certain maximum threshold of growth over a predefined window of tim**e. As a further measure to differentiate a document related to a topical phenomenon from a spam document, **search engine 125 may consider mentions of the document in news articles**, discussion groups, etc. **on the theory that spam documents will not be mentioned, for example, in the news**. Any or a combination of these techniques may be used to curtail spamming attempts.

> *"Thresholds on rankings are used to control how fast pages can rank. Documents are often assigned threshold limits on gains in search engine rankings whereas a document can only move so quickly to the top, although when something is discussed in the "news" it could be naturally expected to generate links more quickly than on average and may become popular, so a document may need to be pushed up quickly. In such instances, a document could be given a 'pass' on normal threshold limits for quick gains in rankings, such as a news event or trending topic."*

[0101] It may be possible for search engine 125 to make exceptions for documents that are determined to be **authoritative in some respect, such as government documents, web directories (e.g., Yahoo),** and documents that have shown a relatively steady and high rank over time. For example, if an unusual spike in the number or rate of increase of links to an authoritative document occurs, then search engine 125 may consider such a document not to be spam and, thus, allow a relatively high or even **no threshold** for (growth of) its rank (over time).

> *"Normal thresholds on pages may be overlooked or given a "free pass" due to trust level. Trusted domains could be able to rank a new document rather quickly because the publisher is trusted."*

[0102] In addition, or alternatively, search engine 125 **may consider significant drops in ranks of documents as an indication that these documents are "out of favor" or outdated**. For example, if the rank of a document over time drops significantly, then search engine 125 may consider the document as outdated and score the document accordingly.

> *"When a document is superseded by other documents which pushes it down (lowers its rankings), it may no longer be considered important or desirable based on the theory that it did not maintain enough use, reference or links to keep it well ranked in search results. Allowing a site to fall in rankings for a period of time could create a trend which could potentially make matters worse."*

[0103] In summary, search engine 125 **may generate (or alter) a score associated with a document based**, at least in part, on information **relating to prior rankings** of the document.

> *"Processes will be used to alter (either positively or negatively) a score of documents or entire domains based on the information related with rankings when measured over a period of time."*

User Maintained/Generated Data

[0104] According to an implementation consistent with the principles of the invention, user maintained or generated data may be used to generate (or alter) a score associated with a document. For example, search engine 125 **may monitor data maintained or generated by a user**, such as "**bookmarks**," "**favorites**," or other types of data that may provide some indication of documents favored by, or of interest to, the user. Search engine 125 may obtain this data either directly (e.g., via a browser assistant) or indirectly (e.g., via a browser). Search engine 125 may then analyze over time a number of bookmarks/favorites to which a document is associated to determine the importance of the document.

> *"A clear indication that bookmarks (the process of adding something to a browsers favorites tab) can be used to alter a score of a document (either positively or negatively) depending on the data gathered on the frequency and number of users who add or remove favorites and bookmarks. This process will attempt to gather this user information either directly from the users browser or some other browser add-on like a browser downloaded plugin or tool bar."*

[0105] Search engine 125 may also analyze upward and downward trends to add or remove the document (or more specifically, a path to the document) from the **bookmarks/favorites lists**, the rate at which the document is added to or removed from the bookmarks/favorites lists, and/or whether the document is added to, deleted from, or accessed through the bookmarks/favorites lists. If a number of users are adding a particular document to their **bookmarks/favorites lists** or **often accessing the document** through such lists over time, this may be considered an indication that the document is relatively important. **On the other hand, if a number of users are decreasingly accessing a document indicated in their bookmarks/favorites list or are increasingly deleting/replacing the path to such document from their lists, this may be taken as an indication that the document is outdated, unpopular, etc. Search engine 125 may then score the documents accordingly.**

> *"Scoring of a document will likely take place based on the frequency of adding or removing bookmarks as well how often the bookmarks are used. Example: Bookmarks used often would be deemed important documents while bookmarks no longer being used often where they were being used often during a prior period of time may be deemed less important and this will affect the score of these documents which will or is likely to affect (either positively or negatively) the documents rankings."*

[0106] In an alternative implementation, **other types of user data that may indicate an increase or decrease in user interest in a particular document over time** may be used by search engine 125 to score the document. For example, **the "temp" or cache files** associated with users could be monitored by search engine 125 to identify whether there is an increase or decrease in a document being added over time. Similarly, **cookies** associated with a particular document might be monitored by search engine 125 to determine whether there is an upward or downward trend in interest in the document.

> *"Cookies from web browsers, temp files, cached files or other types of data from users computers may be used to identify trends and habits which can affect or influence the score of documents."*

[0107] In summary, search engine **125 may generate (or alter) a score** associated with a document based, at least in part, on **user maintained or generated data**.

> *"Processes will be used to alter (either positively or negatively) a score of documents based on the information related with user generated data when measured over a period of time."*

[0108] According to an implementation consistent with the principles of the invention, information regarding **unique words, bigrams, and phrases in anchor text may be used to generate (or alter) a score associated with a document**. For example, search engine 125 may monitor web (or link) graphs and their behavior over time and use this information for scoring, spam detection, or other purposes. **Naturally developed web graphs typically involve independent decisions. Synthetically generated web graphs**, which are usually indicative of an **intent to spam**, are based on coordinated decisions, causing the profile of growth in anchor words/bigrams/phrases to likely be relatively spiky.

> *"Synthetically generated web graphs (SPAM): Varying anchor texts and diversifying placements appears as a more natural behavior so keywords in anchor text are evaluated over periods of time."*

[0109] One reason for such **spikiness may be the addition of a large number of identical anchors from many documents**. Another possibility may be the addition of deliberately different anchors from a lot of documents. Search engine 125 may **monitor the anchors** and factor them into scoring a document to which their associated links point. For example, search engine 125 **may cap the impact of suspect anchors** on the score of the associated document. Alternatively, search engine 125 may use a continuous scale for the likelihood of synthetic generation and derive a multiplicative factor to scale the score for the document.

> *"Synthetic generation (SPAM): Anchor text links may no longer provide credit if a maximum threshold for those anchors has already been met within a period of spikes of such links being acquired. It is important to vary anchor text and link diversity as naturally as possible. Gaining too many links with matching anchor text too fast is a signal of synthetic link generation (a spam attempt)."*

[0110] In summary, search engine 125 may **generate (or alter) a score** associated with a document **based**, at least in **part, on information** regarding unique words, bigrams, and phrases in <u>anchor text</u> associated with one or more links pointing to the document.

> *"Anchor text and link relationships, especially within periods of time where spikes occur in links being acquired can alter (either positively or negatively) the score of a web site or document."*

Linkage of Independent Peers

[0111] According to an implementation consistent with the principles of the invention, information regarding linkage of **independent peers (e.g., unrelated documents)** may be used to generate (or alter) a score associated with a document.

[0112] A **sudden growth** in the number of apparently **independent peers,** incoming and/or outgoing, with a large number of links to individual documents may indicate a potentially synthetic web graph, which is an **indicator of an attempt to spam.** This indication may be strengthened if the growth corresponds to anchor text that is unusually coherent or discordant. **This information can be used to demote the impact of such links,** when used with a link-based scoring technique, either as a binary decision item (e.g., demote the score by a fixed amount) or a multiplicative factor.

[0113] In summary, search engine 125 may **generate (or alter) a score** associated with a document based, at least in part, on **information regarding linkage of independent peers**.

Document Topics

[0114] According to an implementation consistent with the principles of the invention, information regarding **document topics may be used to generate (or alter) a score associated with a document.** For example, search engine 125 may perform topic extraction (e.g., through categorization, URL analysis, content analysis, clustering, summarization, a set of unique low frequency words, or some other type of topic extraction). Search engine 125 may then monitor the topic(s) of a document over time and use this information for scoring purposes.

> *"Document topics, general themes, keywords, and URLs are monitored over periods of time where changes that occur can alter (either positively or negatively) the score of a web site or document."*

[0115] A significant change over time in the set of topics associated with a document may indicate that the **document has changed owners** and previous document indicators, such as score, anchor text, etc., are no longer reliable. Similarly, a spike in the number of topics could indicate spam. For example, if a particular document is associated with a set of one or more topics over what may be considered a "stable" period of time and then a **(sudden) spike occurs in the number of topics associated with the document**, this may be an indication that the document has been taken over as a "doorway" document. Another indication may include the disappearance of the original topics associated with the document. If one or more of these situations are detected, then search engine 125 may reduce the relative score of such documents and/or the links, anchor text, or other data associated the document.

> *"If a document is somewhat steady in topic for a long period of time and suddenly becomes used for multiple new purposes, this could affect the score (either positively or negatively) of the document and any part of the document including links or anchor texts used within the document. Suggests the identification of sites which become possible inventory for links."*

[0116] In summary, search engine 125 **may generate (or alter) a score** associated with a document based, at least in part, on **changes** in one or more **topics** associated with the document.

> *"Change in document "topics" could affect the score (either positively or negatively) of the document and any part of the document including links or anchor texts used within the document."*

Exemplary Processing

[0117] FIG. 4 is a **flowchart of exemplary processing** for **scoring documents** according to an implementation consistent with the principles of the invention. Processing may begin with server 120 identifying documents (act 410). The documents may include, for example, one or more documents associated with a **search query**, such as documents identified as relevant to the search query. Alternatively, the documents may include one or more documents in a corpus or repository of documents that are independent of any search query (e.g., documents that are identified by crawling a network and stored in a repository).

[0118] Search engine 125 **may obtain history data associated with the identified documents** (act 420). As described above, the history data may take different forms. For example, the **history data may include** data relating to document **inception dates;** document **content updates/changes; query analysis; link-based criteria; anchor text; traffic; user behavior; domain-related information; ranking history; user maintained/generated data** (e.g., bookmarks and/or favorites); **unique words, bigrams,** and **phrases in anchor text;** linkage of **independent peers;** and/or document **topics.** Search engine 125 may obtain one, or a combination, of these kinds of history data.

[0119] Search engine 125 may then score the identified documents based, at least in part, on the history data (act 430). **When the identified documents are associated with a search query, search engine 125 may also generate relevancy scores for the documents based, for example, on how relevant they are to the search query.** Search engine 125 may then combine the history scores with the relevancy scores to obtain overall scores for the documents. Instead of combining the scores, search engine 125 may alter the relevancy scores for the documents based on the history data, thereby raising or lowering the scores or, in some cases, leaving the scores the same. Alternatively, search engine 125 may score the documents based on the history data without generating relevancy scores. **In any event, search engine 125 may score the documents using one, or a combination, of the types of history data.**

> *"Documents may be scored by any combination of history data, relevancy data or search query information. Document scores may be altered (either positively or negatively) by either or all."*

[0120] **When the identified documents are associated with a search query, search engine 125 may also form search results from the scored documents.** For example, search engine 125 may sort the documents based on their scores. Search engine 125 may then form references to the documents, where a reference might include a title of the document (which may contain a hypertext link that will direct the user, when selected, to the actual document) and a snippet (i.e., a text excerpt) from the document. In other implementations, the references are formed differently. **Search engine 125 may present references corresponding to a number of the top-scoring documents** (e.g., a predetermined number of the documents, documents with scores above a threshold, all documents, etc.) to a user who submitted the search query.

> *"Processes will display the search results taking information from the pages where deemed relevant and useful to the user which will lead them to the documents (search engine results)."*

CONCLUSION

[0121] Systems and methods consistent with the principles of the invention **may use history data to score documents and form high quality search results**.

> *"Historic data it collects is used to serve high quality search results."*

[0122] The foregoing description of preferred embodiments of the present invention provides illustration and description, but is **not intended to be exhaustive or to limit the invention** to the precise form disclosed. **Modifications and variations are possible in light of the above teachings or may be acquired from practice of the invention.** For example, while a series of acts has been described with regard to FIG. 4, the order of the acts may be modified in other implementations consistent with the principles of the invention. Also, non-dependent acts may be performed in parallel.

> *"The invention uses everything described herein but is not limited to only these disclosed items."*

[0123] Further, it has generally been described that **server 120 performs most, if not all**, of the acts described with regard to the processing of FIG. 4. In another implementation consistent with the principles of the invention, **one or more, or all, of the acts may be performed by another entity**, such as another server 130 and/or 140 or client 110.

> *"The invention processes data as described herein but is not limited to this exact configuration."*

[0124] It will also be apparent to one of **ordinary skill in the art that aspects of the invention, as described above, may be implemented in many different forms** of software, firmware, and hardware in the implementations illustrated in the figures. The actual software code or specialized control hardware used to implement aspects consistent with the principles of the invention is not limiting of the present invention. Thus, **the operation and behavior of the aspects were described without reference to the specific software code--it being understood that one of ordinary skill in the art would be able to design software and control hardware to implement the aspects based on the description herein.**

> *"The entire invention as well as its processing, storage and configuration is based upon software and hardware elements consistent with the illustrations and descriptions herein, but it is to be understood that any software, hardware or skill not specifically referenced here could be used and/or used to complete the art of the invention as described within these claims."*

Chapter 30 (Google's +1 Feature Poised to Take Over)

Google released its Google+ network in July of 2011 and in just one month it was estimated to have twenty million users. Those who understand the significance of Google +1 see the writing on the wall, and those who don't will soon follow suit.

Here is a few reasons why I predict +1 will continue to grow – and grow quickly.

1 – When people click +1, their connections will find those pages easier.

Not everyone realizes it yet, but once people hit the +1 button either on Google or an actual web page, that page automatically becomes more relevant to those who are connected to you through Google services like Gmail or Google's social network. This can result in a huge traffic increase for those whose sites generate a lot of +1 activity. For example, if you are connected to 50 people and you +1 a page, those 50 people are more likely to find that page when searching. If any of those 50 people hit +1, the same will happen with their connections – and so on. It's like a revolving traffic MLM program for the Internet.

2 – More and more people will learn about +1 as well as rely on +1s over time.

Whenever something is fresh and/or new it takes time for it to become accepted with the general public. Facebook, Twitter, Digg, Myspace, etc., all went through their own growing pains for initial years until they were widely accepted by the masses. This process will be significantly different with Google +1, in my opinion. Google has an uncanny reach and acceptability factor with those who already use the search engine. Also, Google+ is already integrated with everything Google offers. The dominance Google has held in the search space has been unlike anything anyone has seen in such competitive spaces of business such as 'advertising' and 'technology'. Allowing people to influence Google's powerful search engine will be the rocket-launcher for Google+ and +1s popularity.

3 – Sites with +1 activity will see better rankings.

This just makes plain old good sense. Overtime, Google will use +1 activity to influence its normal algorithm whether a user is signed in for search or not. Sites with heavy +1 activity will be deemed more important and vice versa. More and more traffic will be rewarded to better sites while webmasters will begin to cater more to their users rather than search engines. Google's Webmaster Tools control panel is showing +1 activity including clicks and influence. If your site is getting +1 activity Google Webmaster Tools will show you all about it. Below is an example of what you'll see (if you're getting +1's that is).

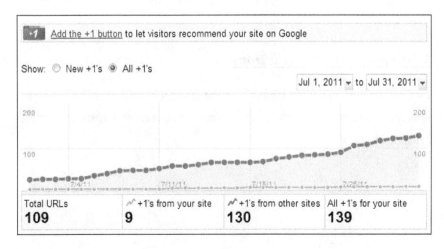

4 – Spam sites and low quality pages will just go away.

Google has felt the pressure with cleaning up the Internet for some time now. After all, what ranks well on Google people find and what doesn't rank, well, you need a road map to get to. Is Google responsible for what people do or don't see online? Some people feel that they are and although in reality Google is just a great tool for those who seek information, they are often the "be-all" "end-all" for what gets seen.

This shifts, what I'm sure is, some unwanted responsibility on their end and Google has been molding its algorithm to cater more to "brand authority" when it comes to what web sites come up and which do not. Just as people trust brands, so does Google. Within the last year or so, established brands have been stealing the rankings of many smaller, newer sites and this isn't going to change too much – because people like brands, people often need brands and at the end of the day, brands will warrant +1s from users.

When all is said and done, sites not 'liked' by users (measured by +1 activity) which don't acquire +1 activity will just go away. Google wins again.

Want my official prediction?

Google will eventually tie every web site on the Internet back to a specific 'person' or 'author', otherwise it just won't rank that well on Google.com.

Chapter 31 (Focusing On The Future)

Considering the many different ways that Google examines the millions of documents which make up the Internet, it continually seems more evident and important that web site operators who wish to be found online must consistently build, market, maintain and promote their web sites in order to maintain the freshness and value sophisticated search engines like Google are looking for.

It is also increasing unlikely that search will just go away. As advertising revenues for print newspapers fell to a record low in 2011 of $4.75 billion, advertiser placements on the Internet rose sharply. Web advertising revenues for the first quarter of 2011 were 23 percent higher than those for the first quarter of the previous year, attaining a high point of $7.3 billion. This reflects the shifting habits of Americans, who are increasingly comfortable with using the web for shopping and product selection for brick-and-mortar purchases in addition to the more conventional purposes of entertainment and research.

So it's clear that search isn't going anywhere soon, and search optimization will continue to be a necessary component for some time to come – it's just changing and getting harder to do over time.

What worries me most of all, with regard to the net, is online privacy, threats from hackers, security as well as the increased legislation, interest in taxation and scrutiny of the Internet by U.S. House Representatives and Senators as well as what seems like a fundamental lack of understanding and compassion for the importance of network neutrality - a principle that advocates no restrictions by Internet service providers (ISP's) or governments on consumers' access to networks that participate in the Internet.

But that's all for another book. As far as optimization, sites will continue the need to find ways to generate their own new value, freshness, buzz and links, to avoid being "superseded by another document". The one and only way to effectively avoid promoting your web site as a fundamental need of doing business online would be to develop and build a web site which becomes so "massively great" that it does its own marketing via true reporting, user need, interest, popularity and buzz.

As the web is also becoming more socially connected every day, Google's insatiable appetite for user data signals a shift towards more evaluation of user interaction with web sites meaning webmasters must focus greatly on the usability of their sites, features, functionality and whatever will keep users interested and engaged with their content.

The power of the social web should not be underestimated by any means. Twitter, Facebook and Google+ appear to be the leading players out of all social networks but this could change quickly, especially with rising stars like Pinterest, the social network specifically for sharing images (pins).

So what's next? What's to come down the road?

Google places will compete for all Yellow Pages style businesses worldwide and listings will be verifiable. Google+ will begin to compete and possibly surpass leading social sites like Facebook and Twitter due to the power of Google's intermingling services like Gmail and YouTube. Google Analytics, a neat tool which seemed like a free perk from the ole' GOOG, will be installed across every site that exists because eventually sites will do better when Google knows more - and now watch how quick people jump on the bandwagon when they notice the effect "authorship" has on their posts (it's going to be big!). Google will eventually tie every single site back to a unique individual via a Google+ Profile. And all of this will be used to rank the results, and for your own good of course. I mean, in order to make search better for you, they need to know YOU a little better – right??

Also, don't forget, the more complicated and unpredictable the results become, the more business owners will resort to PPC. If I had to take a guess, I'd say Google's second quarter revenues this year will see a spike in a positive direction, another win for the ole GOOG. You've got to hand it to them over there, they really know what they're doing.

As far as I see it, Google is clearly winning the war, not just in "Search", but in life itself. Google knows you (through your searches), your friends (through your connections), your likes (with Google+), their likes (with Search Plus Your World), what entertains you (through YouTube) or what makes you laugh – or cry, where you are in the world at any given time (through Gmail and your Android phone) or where you've been – and I bet with a relatively low amount of computing power – Google even knows where you're going before you get there. Maybe Google will predict your next action, your next thought based on a collaboration of thoughts past?

Wishing you good luck!

"I hope that this book has provided you with valuable insight and has built added confidence in your ability for "Mastering Your Website". Knowledge and strategy is everything, especially when doing business online.

I will leave you with this final thought. With everything I have seen change over the years, don't make the mistake of focusing only on search engines and site optimization. Focus on your users; your brand; build an immensely great site; an absolutely awesome resource - and keep improving it as best you can.

*Search engines are looking to deliver great sites – **be great!"***

All the best,
John Colascione
Searchen Networks ® Inc.

www.ingramcontent.com/pod-product-compliance
Lightning Source LLC
Chambersburg PA
CBHW071426050326
40689CB00010B/2002